ELENI F

&

THE BURNED SOUL

(2)

Message from the author.

As soon as you record an idea, for example by writing down the outline of a story, it's protected by copyright. As long as the work is original, copyright protection is automatic. Copyright ensures works cannot be reproduced or used without your permission.

So, with that in mind, I am putting this in writing that this is my work and with the exception of quotations that can be used in reviews. No part of these novels may be reproduced or shared in any form without written and recorded consent from myself - The Author.

Thank you.

PROLOGUE

*The Headmaster dragged the redhead out from her prison
into the lashing rain by her hair. The woman let out a muffled
whine as he rammed a wooden stake right through her heart.
Without a second's hesitation, before she had a chance to beg
for mercy, he begun slashing at her throat, over and over
with his blade, and through such ferocity, her head
dethatched from her body with a sickening crunch. His final
act, before returning to the hospital, was setting her ablaze
with his magic and watching her decapitated body burn to
dust . . .*

1- LAST WORD HEARD.

I floated under. I drifted gently. I dreamed.

Dark water swirled around me. I was gravity-stricken, weightless, non-submersible, rootless in the blackness as my body wafted motionless through the abyss.

A happy tone then suddenly muffled through the thick inky fogged-water, and gently trickled into my ears. It was the sweetest lullaby my mind could conjure up. It was beautiful and uplifting. I was brought back, almost to the surface, by a sharp twinge ripping up my leg. Despite the soaring slashing-pain coursing my thigh, I couldn't find my way back far enough to open my eyes. My throat had been slit, my artery in my leg severed. There was no return for me now.

I knew I was dead. I had to be dead. Here I was floating into nothing, just darkness, and yet I could hear this angel's voice calling my name as I drifted leisurely through the bleak.

"Stay with me Eleni," the angel's voice cried in horror through the blackness.

That longed-for lullaby-voice continued to call my name, but behind it in the distance, almost out of reach from my ears, was the cry of a muffled woman. Her speech slurred as though she couldn't move her jaw.

"Eleni!" The alluring voice called out again, drowning out the horrible background slur of the other woman, "Eleni, please open your eyes!"

I tried to answer, I tried so hard. But I couldn't locate my lips. My body wouldn't respond.

"Jade. Sofia. Help me heal her. We may already be too late!" The angel called out - agony in her faultless voice.

Other voices swirled around me now. Not nowhere near as sweet, but still friendly and worried. I could hear cries and sobs. This couldn't be heaven? Angels shouldn't be crying. I thought I recognised the voices, and I so wanted to reach out and find them to tell them that it was ok, but my mind drifted slowly away again peacefully, and all was nearly forgotten in my dark empty bliss.

"Place your hands on her side and let me guide you both," that lullaby voice trickled into my ear again like warm honey.

I looked around to try and locate where it was coming from, but I was just surrounded by nothing, a black hole of emptiness and darkness.

"I could hear the other voices sobbing," this wasn't right.

I tried to locate them, but the water was too deep. I couldn't find the surface and I wasn't sure which way was up or which way was down. I looked for the air bubbles to see which way they were floating, but there were none. The tar-coloured water was thick and pressing on me, I couldn't breathe.

All of a sudden the blackness around me turned white, the water had changed colour - but only around me. Purple and blue flowed through it as it surrounded me, almost like a hand grabbing me and tugging me upwards. I was still in the black water, but this blue and purple light had cradled me, shielding me from the gloom. Pressure shot against me and I could feel pain in my head and then my leg. It was agonising pain that got stronger and stronger the more the purple and blue ocean engulfed me. Wrapping me up like a blanket. I twisted round and round in the water as the current continued to drag me. My pains were getting stronger to the point that I couldn't take it anymore. I cried out, screaming, panicking, splashing, fighting for my life suddenly as the black tried to pull me from the purple glow. I felt gripped by two forces, almost as though they were playing tug of war and I was the rope. I pushed with all my might, kicking my legs and gasping, finally breaking through the dark pool and into the purple light. My eyes shot open. Everything had gone from complete blackout to complete white. My eyes blinked and shut for a moment, returning to the blackness before opening and returning to the white. Either way I couldn't see, and the white realm was just as terrifying as the black realm. It had gone from complete darkness to a white fog.

"Eleni!" That perfect angel's voice cried out.

Had I made it to heaven? My eyesight couldn't focus; I still struggled to fully open my eyes. The fog was beginning to subside and clear.

Suddenly a manly voice broke the lullaby.

"Eleni, please! Eleni, listen to me, please, please, Eleni, please!" The voice begged.

I wanted to respond, but nothing came out.

"Indira!" The manly voice called in agony, "Eleni, Eleni, no, oh please, don't let this happen, please! No, no!!!"

My eyes finally begun to focus as the fog drifted away.

"Eleni!" That lullaby angel voice trickled, but the perfect voice was crying, "She's lost a lot of blood!"

"Is she going to be alright?" That manly voice wept. "Please tell me that she is going to be alright?"

"I don't know. My magic can only do so much when someone has been hurt this much. She's in a bad way," the perfect voice replied.

A howl of rage ripped from the manly voice, "Bring the prisoner to me!"

"I vith noth speath," a strange voice spoke; it was the slur I had heard previously in the distance.

"I don't want you to speak. A broken jaw is the least of your worries right now. I want you to know that if she dies, then you will suffer a fate far worse than death. My wrath knows no limits!" The manly voice was enraged with fury, "Get her out of my sight!"

"Yes, headmaster," a raspy voice replied. A sexy voice – I recognised *that* voice.

"Linx!" I gasped.

"She's awake!!!" The lullaby voice yelled.

Suddenly everyone was speaking at once, "Eleni! Eleni!"

I blinked as I took in the images. I was surrounded by Indira, my father, Sofia, Stephanie, Jade, Dotty, Estella . . . *and* . . . oh that beautiful boy . . . Linx.

"Give her some space," Indira's calming voice soothed the air. Everyone slowly backed away, except my father and Inidra.

"Dad," I tried to tell him, but my voice was thick and heavy and sluggish. I couldn't understand my own slow words.

"Eleni, you're going to be ok. Can you hear me, Eleni? I love you too."

"Daddy," I tried again. My voice now finally clearing.

"Yes, I'm here sweetheart. Daddy is here."

"It hurts," I whimpered.

"I know baby, I know."

"Daaaad," I wheezed as everything started to go black again.

"She's fading!" Father barked.

"Linx, come here!" Indira's lovely voice demanded, "Hold her hand and speak to her."

"Why?" My father protested, he sounded appalled.

"*Because* when she heard his voice she woke up and whispered his name," Indira replied, "If he can keep her awake for long enough I may be able to save her. She's lost so much blood. We may have to take her to a hospital."

"And how will we explain this to the hospital, all the stab wounds and the slit throat?" Father argued.

My head spun wildly.

"We will need to warp their minds afterwards," Indira suggested.

"That'll use up so many power stones. It'll weaken us dramatically in our fight to stop Jealousaw from breaching the shields and entering Earth!" Father growled.

"What's more important right now?" Indira snapped.

"Keep her awake, Linx. I'll get the car!" Father grumbled. His voice sounded strained.

My eyes were nearly closed now, but something warm touched my hand. I felt a jolt of electricity shoot up me from his warm touch and my eyes fluttered through the darkness, slowly opening. I knew I was smiling like an idiot, but I didn't care, I was so happy to see him. His cool fingers brushed at the wetness in my eyes. "Hello," I drooled, he was *so* handsome.

"The healing powers have similar affects to those on morphine," Indira explained to Linx as he was bewildered by my lustful flirtatious grin at him.

I was so tired though, I had to sleep, I needed to sleep.

"Eleni! Stay awake!" Linx gasped. I couldn't see his face as everything started going dark.

"Keep talking to her. You *must* not let her pass out again," Indira warned.

"Tell me about your farm," Linx tried.

I wanted to reply but I was drifting.

"What's your full name. I don't know it?" Indira cut in.

"I don't know my middle name," I wheezed.

"What's your surname?" Linx asked quickly.

"Fox," I mumbled exhaustedly, *why won't they let me sleep?*

"I have the car!" Fathers voice roared.

"Quickly, we haven't got long. She's dying!" Indira's voice caught in her throat as she yelled.

I heard father catch his breath in horror.

Suddenly I was in Linx's strong arms. I writhed in his grip as my entire body throbbed in pain. The movement was making my leg flare sickeningly. I realised my eyes were shut again. I opened them, desperate to find him. Finally there he was. His perfect face, staring back at me, twisted into a mask of indecision and pain.

"Get her in the car!" Father ordered.

Suddenly Linx's expression changed, his drawn face that was full of doubt lit up with a blaze of determination. His jaw tightened. "You're going to be alright!" His voice was determined as he placed me on the backseat.

"I'll take the girls back to their dorms," Indira's perfect voice spoke.

"We love you Eleni," Stephanie, Dotty, Estella, Sofia and Jade cried out in the distance as the car door slammed shut.

My head was on Linx's lap, and father roared the car to life. Linx kept talking to me for the entire journey and we took so many sharp turns, father was driving fast! I loved looking into Linx's eyes, but it was time to sleep now.

"Eleni!!!" Linx gasped, and that was the last word I heard.
"ELENI!!!!!!!"

2- *INVITATIONS*

Falling down the stairs like that at Estella's birthday party was so clumsy. Me and all the girls constantly joke about it, although none of us can quite fully remember, as apparently we were all a little drunk. We all were held in detention for a few days - after I had recovered - for being outside the school grounds without telling anybody, and for underage drinking. Estella was relieved that we weren't expelled. That was the least of my concerns though. There was only one thing on my mind.

I had dreamt about Lingwood every night since I got out of the hospital. It started off with me just having a normal dream and suddenly he'd be in it, walking past me or standing in the distance glaring those gorgeous eyes at me. Then as the nights progressed and the dreams continued, I'd find that they got more intense. It started with him standing over my bed and I'd wake up sweating. Then we were holding hands walking down the beach. Then he would kiss me. And the same dreams went on and on, intensifying more and more.

The month that followed was a little uneasy, tense, and most certainly embarrassing. To my horror and dismay I found myself the centre of attention for the rest of that first week after my trip to hospital after the demon attack, and then my second trip to the hospital practically the following week from falling down the stairs drunk at Estella's birthday celebrations - apparently, although my memory was a little fuzzy on that one. Courtesy of those two trips to the hospital everybody was now impossible, following me around, obsessed with how I was feeling. It was a nightmare. My anger towards Lingwood eased slightly as I begun to feel a sense of gratitude that he put his body in-between mine and that creature when I ended up in hospital the first time round. But the way we had left things made things awkward, and he avoided me like the plague. I wanted very much to try and talk to him. We had left things so bad. We were both so furious the last time we had talked outside the hospital. If truth be told the heat of my anger was fading more and more into aw gratitude at my saviour. As pitiful, pathetic and cliché as it sounded, he was my hero, my knight in shining armour. And now he hated me. Probably regretted saving me too.

I sighed as we had an unavoidable class together and our seats were next to each other. I sat down, expecting some sort of response, or at least a slight turn towards me, but he showed no sign that he had even realised I was there.

"Hi," I said nicely, trying to show him that things were fine as I tried to provoke a pleasant response.

He barely turned his head a fraction and nodded once before looking away. He didn't even look at me. And that was the last contact we had. I found myself watching him sometimes from a distance. But every class that we had, where unfortunately we had to sit next to one another, we acted as though the other didn't exist. I was so miserable, especially as I couldn't get him out of my mind. The dreams about him still continued every night, but this time no intimacy or passion. He'd just stand there in the distance looking at me, or he'd be walking and I'd be struggling to catch him up. I'd always wake up sweating.

The snow and icy weather from a few weeks back had completely dried up now, or rather washed away with all the heavy rain and thunderstorms we had. The trip to 'The Grey-Beach Water Resort' that Stephanie had planned still couldn't go ahead just yet due to the heavy rainfall, but the forecast was stating that conditions would be soon dry. So at least that could be something to look forward to.

Linx informed me that our defensive Space-station got wiped out, which means our shields are weakened - but still they remained strong somehow, just keeping Jealousaw at bay. For now. But there had been no contact from Lukamore. This news deeply saddened me.

My birthday came and I turned 17. Father sent me a card to my room and a chocolate birthday cake, but still couldn't grace me with his presence. I did receive a nice birthday text from my mum along with a special card in the post that had a picture of Fiona in it, which made me cry. Oh how I missed my horse.

Sofia, Dotty, Jade, Estella and Stephanie snuck some alcohol into our room in the early hours of the morning and we had a nice girlie night. But the real highlight was earlier on, when Linx took me out for a meal. Despite a few nice smiles sent my way and us getting on great, I knew not to read into anything and read signs wrong. I just enjoyed his company as friends. Training with him everyday had been so professional and robotic, that it was nice to just go out together and act normal. The real downer was that me and Lingwood still hadn't spoken a word all week, and soon more weeks passed by.

Now a month had passed and Stephanie made me aware of the upcoming school dance that was fast approaching, and remained very persistent when I told her that I wouldn't be attending.

"No, Stepth, I'm not going," I assured her. Dancing was something I had never done and never intended on doing.

"Don't be silly, you'll definitely be coming, it'll be fun," she tried.

"I don't have a date, and I doubt anyone will ask me. You go have fun," I encouraged.

The next day I was sitting in class next to Lingwood as usual, and as usual he didn't even glance my way.

"Hi, I'm Mike," a boy said as he approached our desk, almost as though he had heard me and Stephanie somehow psychically the previous night. *Or Stephanie had arranged it* – I thought sceptically. I noticed that Lingwood twitched slightly out of the corner of my eye.

"Hi, I'm Eleni," I replied cheerfully.

The boy sat awkwardly at the edge of our desk.

"So, err, I was wondering," he stuttered nervously. "Do you have anyone to go to the dance with?"

I paused my response, hating the ocean of guilt whose waves crashed and splashed my insides, but, I saw from the corner of my eye; Lingwood's head tilt my way.

"I'm sorry, I'm not planning on going, but my friend Dotty really likes you, and she hasn't got a date to the dance," I assured, feeling a little guilty that I palmed him off on Dotty. Then shock horror shot through me as I realised I had just set him up for another rejection, as Dotty was gay. "Or Sofia," I quickly said, then realised I had set him up for a brutal rejection. *STOP!* – I commanded to myself inside my head; - *just let the boy walk away.*

"Oh," he mumbled as he tried to act cool, but his face was bright red and I could see in his eyes how dejected and embarrassed he felt.

"Perhaps I'll ask her then," he said as he walked off with his head hung low.

I closed my eyes and sighed as I pressed my fingers to my temples. I felt so guilty. I was flattered that I had been asked, but I was suffering from slight depression lately and the last thing I needed was this stupid dance. When I opened my eyes Lingwood was staring at me curiously with his black eyes. I glared back, surprised, expecting him to look away, but he didn't. His eyes were intense and sexy and I felt tingly and scared. My hands trembled and there was no way I could hold his stare. I quickly glanced away shyly. Finally his eyes released me as he looked out of the window. I couldn't believe the bolts of emotions that ran through me like a current – just because he so happened to look at me for the first time in a month. I knew this wasn't healthy, or sane, to let someone have this level of influence over me and it was a little pathetic, pitiful even. I focused all of my energies into not noticing him and tried so hard not to glance out of the corner of my eye, but that proved impossible, so instead I made sure he wasn't aware of my little peeks, something girls were way better at doing, than guys.

I sighed embarrassingly loudly with relief when the bell chimed to end the class. I turned my back to him to gather my things, expecting him to leave like he always did.

"Eleni," his deep sexy voice called my name.

I gulped and turned slowly and unwillingly, desperately trying not to look at his too-perfect-face.

"What do you want?" I snapped unintentionally as a rush of emotions pulsed through me.

"I just wanted to say Happy Birthday for last month," he said as he flashed his perfect teeth, "I'm sorry I missed it."

My eyes narrowed, "You're suddenly talking to me to wish me happy birthday, nearly four weeks late!" I gritted my teeth, holding back the anger.

His lips twitched slightly and he clearly didn't know what to say.

"I'm sorry," he sounded sincere, but what he then said next killed the genuine apology dead in the water. "But us not being friends is for the best."

My eyebrows stooped almost vertically, "You should have just saved yourself all this stress Lingwood and let that demon get me!" I gushed angrily, emotionally, and a little hatefully.

"Stress?" He was astonished and glared at me in disbelief, "You think me saving you, causes me stress?"

"Yeah! You should have just let me die mate!" I growled.

He paused for a minute, clearly taken by surprise and caught off guard by my hostile approach, but what did he really expect from a girl that he has blanked for a month? When he finally did muster up the courage to speak, he sounded angry.

"I'd never let any harm come to you!"

"Whatever!" I snarled without looking up at his gorgeous face out of fear that his handsomeness would steel my thunder.

I wanted to stay mad at him, he deserved this, and if I allowed myself to look, then I knew his charming smile and lustful eyes would win me over. I had to stay strong, I'm better than this, and deserve to be treated better than this. I turned my head away from him sharply and gathered my books whilst

clenching my jaw. I wanted to lash out at him and shout and
scream and call him every name under the sun, but I could feel
the tears behind my eyes building and just needed to get out of
there before I embarrassed myself. I grabbed my stuff and
rushed towards the exit, but typically I caught my elbow on the
door and my books plummeted out of my hands, crashing to
the floor. I sighed and considered leaving them, but decided to
quickly bend down and gather them up hastily. As soon as I
knelt down he was there, and he was rapidly sorting them into
a neat pile for me. I went to grab the last book just as he had,
and his hand ended up on top of mine. The electricity that shot
through me made my entire body tingle at his cold touch. I
retreated my hand sharply, and he picked up the pile of books,
handing them to me.

"Thanks," I hissed icily as I snatched them off of him.

"You're welcome," he retorted.

I gulped, straightened up stiffly, and shot out the door like
lightening, getting as far away from him and as quickly as I
could.

Training with Linx that day was brutal. I had come on in leaps
and bounds and he said that I was almost ready to go on my
first 'Stone Chaser' mission with him. That filled me with
excitement, but the training that day seemed the hardest yet. I
kept losing my footing and balance as my mind was so filled

with Lingwood. I tried to concentrate, but he kept creeping back into my thoughts and throwing me off-balance.

"So, I've heard that you, Jade, Estella, Dotty, Stephanie and Sofia make quite the team. The headmaster thinks that you girls have the most potential he's witnessed in decades," Linx complimented as he ceased our training.

"Thanks," I grinned as I regained my breath.

"But you seem somewhat distracted today, is everything alright?"

"I'm fine," I sighed, "Just nervous for the fight that is heading our way soon." It wasn't a lie at all, I really was nervous about the battle with Jealousaw, who wouldn't be? - But I left out the part about Lingwood being on my mind.

"Well, you girls actually stand a chance if you continue to train hard. I've heard Stephanie is becoming very powerful with her control over fire magic," he said, keeping up the illusion that any of us stood a chance.

He was a terrible liar and I could always tell when he was pulling off a fib, but I wasn't going to call him out on it as I understood why he was doing it. It's important to keep spirits high. After all, if Winston Churchill didn't tell a few porkpies to keep up appearances and keep spirits high, then England would have fallen into panic and chaos during World War times, and who knows what could have happened. Plus, it got inside Hitler's head, this delusional Prime Minister that thinks Britain is winning. Some would argue he lied to the nation, but history speaks for itself on that one, he understood the importance of hope and motivation. I was a huge Winston fan after I watched that movie *'Darkest Hour.'* I figured I'm a little bias as I love the actor *'Gary Oldman.'* That was until me and mum watched *'The Crown'* on Netflix and I realised it was in fact the character Winston who I had a fascination for. *'John Lithgow'* did a great job playing an older Churchill in that. Not that I'm comparing Linx to Winston Churchill. That really would be absurd. He's more like some sort of warrior superhero with big sexy muscles and a cute face, rather than an overweight alcoholic in a top-hat with a cigar.

"Stephanie is great with fire magic," I replied, "but she isn't so great with the sword fighting part." I shrugged, finally answering his question, after my brain going off on one of its adventures about Winston Churchill.

"Well, you're a great sword-fighter, so you'll make a good team. Plus, Dotty is a 'Stone-Lord,' so she has super strength and a heavy stone sword that can break any blade, if struck hard enough," he reminded me.

"That's true, but she lacks conviction and doubts herself too much," I challenged.

"But Sofia is an 'Ice-Lord' and lacks no conviction," he answered quickly. "There is a reason we paired you lot up, you know. Your friendship makes you powerful, and your strengths counter each other's weaknesses."

"But Sofia is ruthless and reckless. Her anger gets the better of her," I disputed.

"Like I said, *your* strengths and weaknesses as a team balance each other out. Sofia has you girls to keep her grounded and calm," he clarified.

I nodded, "And what about Estella, she is a 'Wood-Fairy', how does a magic wooden sword that controls plants, help us? – What use are plants?" I was clearly in an argumentative mood now.

Linx smirked but didn't laugh, "Have you seen Batman?" He asked randomly.

I frowned, "Which film?"

"Batman and Robin."

"Yeah I watched it," I said with an even deeper frown as I wasn't sure where he was heading.

"Poison Ivy," he shrugged with a smile, "Don't underestimate plant power Eleni, and besides, Estella's wooden sword can't be chopped by anything. That wooden sword can hold it's own against steel-metal-blades," he explained.

"Ok, and what about Jade then?" I smirked playfully.

"Jade is a 'Master of Unicorns' and the prophecy that Jealousaw wants to destroy. Her pink and white flamed sword is the most powerful out of everything, but there is no way she can engage in battle with Jealousaw. You girls have to protect her at all costs," he lectured.

"And the sword with the crystal handle that I wasn't allowed to touch?" I raised my eyebrow and smiled cheekily at him.

He sighed and smirked back, "That is a 'Time Peer of the realm' sword and can only be wielded by a 'Time Aristocrat', and they don't exist anymore."

"Why?" I knew I was pushing my luck now with the questions, but that sword did call out to me.

"Time-Magic could only be wielded by very few, and once the magic was banished, they slowly over the years became extinct. There hasn't been 'A Time Aristocrat' for centuries," he expressed.

"Why was the magic banished?"

"Time shouldn't be messed with," Was his blunt response.

"That sword called out to me Linx," I blurted.

His facial expression dropped to worry.

"That's not possible Eleni," he said with determination to his tone.

"Well it did," I shrugged.

"Then you should speak to Indira," he said with a nod. Terror expressed across his face.

"Are you ok?" I asked, feeling worried by his sudden look of horror.

"Well," he sighed as he placed one hand onto his hip and the other to his head, running his fingers through his thick black and grey hair. "If that sword did call to you, then you shouldn't be able to wield 'The Stone Chaser' sword." He paused and I could see by his facial expression that he wasn't finished, but he was struggling to say it. "Only two people in history have ever been known to wield two different magic's," he gulped. "Well, guess I could be the third," I meant it as a joke but he didn't laugh. Instead he turned to me worry stricken as pale as a ghost, like he was about to be sick as panic flared all over his features. "You don't understand Eleni," he paused again in deep thought and dread. "The only two people ever to be able to wield two powers is 'The Burned Soul' and Jealousaw," his voice quivered slightly as he said it.

"Are you trying to say I'm going to turn evil?" I gasped, half joking and half terrified.

He turned and grabbed my hand with his. The warm touch of our skin sent tingles through my body and suddenly Lingwood was gone from my thoughts.

"You could never be evil. Not you!" He said with grit determination as though he were trying to convince me . . . or perhaps himself.

Suddenly he hugged me tight and I hugged him back. When we broke away I could sense that he didn't want to let our bodies detach from the clasp. I glanced up into his green-blue eyes. His hot breath mixed with mine as our eyes locked intensely for a moment. I knew he wanted to kiss me just as I wanted to kiss him, but he backed away at the last minute as our lips drew near.

"Training is over for today," he sounded relieved.

I took a step back and nodded silently without saying a word, trying to keep my poker face strong as disappointment seeped from my pours.

"Indira and the headmaster will know what to do," he reassured. "Get back to your dorm and I'll inform them."

"Ok," I mumbled with a quick flash of a smile before I ran off back to my room.

My brain now wrestled with the two boys, what was wrong with me? I'm not *that* desperate for male attention, otherwise I would have accepted that random boys offer to go to the dance with him. I couldn't even remember his blasted name. No, for some absurd reason I was obsessed with Lingwood and Linx! I could scream at my stupidity. Neither guy wanted me. Lingwood clearly could sense how pathetically attracted to him I was, so absorbed by him, that he was repelled enough to not even want to be friends with me. - I almost sobbed there and then, but I pulled it together. And, as for Linx, he clearly felt something but was held back by my age, or again was that all in my head? Was all of this in my head? A stupid ridiculous fantasy, – I thought angrily, – Of course they weren't interested in me. I wasn't interesting like they were. I wasn't brilliant . . . mysterious . . . perfect . . . and beautiful in every single way, like they were. - *FINE!* – I snarled angrily inside my head, I could leave them alone, I *would* leave them alone. I stomped around my room in a huff.

The next morning I had woken in the same temper-tantrum I had gone to sleep with. Stupid boys! I frowned as I walked to school.

Suddenly from nowhere Lingwood was walking alongside me. I jumped with fright as his sudden appearance startled me.

"How do you do that?" I growled with amazed irritation.

"Do what?" He smirked cheekily and I refused to look at him.

"Just appear like that? Out of thin air!" I grumbled, if my frown got any lower then my eyebrows would be touching the tip of my nose.

"Eleni, it's not my fault you are unbelievably unobservant," he chuckled which only added more fuel to my fire.

I finally frowned at his perfect face. His eyes were black and mysterious with a slight tinge of red. I had to look down. My thoughts were devastatingly tangled at this moment in time.

"What happened to being terrified of my dad?" I said bitterly as I remembered our heated conversation outside the hospital, still looking away.

"Oh, I figured you're worth it!" He snickered.

"You think I'm *worth it*!" I screamed, "You acted like I didn't exist. . . YOU . . ." I couldn't think of a bad enough word to shout at him to calm the anger that raged and burned within me. So I ended up saying nothing and just making a growl noise as I stomped away, sloshing angrily through the rain. He seemed even more amused by my temper as he followed me.

"I'm not pretending you don't exist, that would be impossible," he called out with a slight chuckle to his voice.

I ignored him and carried on walking.

"Wait!" He begged.

I continued to ignore him and marched on in my rage. But he was suddenly next to me, easily keeping pace with my stomp.

"Why won't you leave me alone?" I sighed, caught somewhere between anger and distraught.

"I wanted to ask you a question," he said seriously.

"Make it quick, I'm late for class!" I grumbled.

"Would you go to the dance with me?"

"Are you joking?" I wheeled towards him with such rage that I thought for a second I was going to punch him. My hair and eyes getting drenched as I scowled up at his smug expression, his gorgeous eyes were wickedly amused.

"You think this is funny!" I shouted as I pushed his chest, not expecting it to be so firm and so perfect and so muscular. I refocused my anger. "The answer is no!" I shouted as I pushed him again.

"Ok," he said calmly.

My eyes raged at his smugness.

"What do you mean *ok*?" I growled as I shoved him again.

"What do you want me to say?" He chuckled, looking at me as though I was mad.

Rage radiated from me. "You're unbelievable," I shouted as I pushed him again. This time he grabbed my arms to stop me.

"I'm sorry," he said sincerely, looking me right in the face.

I could feel the tears soaking my eyes and the anger seeping frustratingly away. He doesn't deserve my forgiveness, but looking at his perfect face certainly wasn't helping my clarity of angry thoughts against him.

"I'm tired of trying to stay away from you. I've tried so hard. God I have tried!" He asserted. His eyes were intense and his voice was smouldering. I suddenly couldn't remember how to breathe as my breath paused in my throat.

"Please come to the dance with me," he said passionately.

I couldn't speak yet, so I just nodded.

He nodded too. "We really should stay away from each other," he warned, "But I can't!"

I wanted to say *me neither*, but my voice had gone missing with complete shock.

"I'll see you in class," he said as he rushed off.

I stood there dazed for a few moments until my wrist started to pulse aggressively.

"Oh crap!" I sighed as the pain in my wrist begun to burn more and more. "I'm late for class!" *That awful magic the teachers use to burn your wrists to remind you to never skip class! Bloody abusers!* But, something other than the wrist magic was abusing me now, abusing my thoughts. I couldn't get my bearings as confusion shot through me. I felt dizzy and light headed and my stomach twisted in knots. I don't even remember making the walk to class as I strolled around in a daze.

Later that day I was sitting at lunch with the girls.

"There was another animal attack last night in the town just outside the castle walls. Apparently the bodies were ripped to shreds with all the blood missing," Dotty told excitedly.

"Oh my god!" Jade gasped.

"Why don't they just move all the townsfolk behind the castle walls, they'd be safe here?" I asked stupidly.

Everyone sniggered and I went a little red.

"This castle blocks the gates to hell, which is a massive secret. Could you imagine the amount of devil-worshipers and Satanists we'd get come around here if it leaked out? Not to mention the press and the conspiracy theorists - and that's not even mentioning the magic that is located here. You'd get scientists trying to prove and find a logical reason and explanation to everything. Not to mention the men in white coats that would try to take us away. Plus the governments will want to take over, try to abuse the power in some way to benefit them. This is why the gates stay shut and we hide behind these stupid walls. Nobody comes in from outside, not unless they're in on the secret. The world isn't ready, not sure if it ever will be. That's why this castle is hidden," Sofia grumbled.

We all sort of went quiet, not knowing what to say.

"I saw Lingwood talking to you," Stephanie giggled, changing the subject.

Sofia sent a burning glare my way.

"Yes," I confirmed.

"Well?" Stephanie said.

"He asked me to the dance," I mumbled, trying not to smirk.

All the girls giggled and screeched with excitement, except Sofia who just shook her head at me. Jade had picked up on her disapproving glare.

"What's got *your* knickers in a twist?" Jade spat.

Estella came to her defence, "We told her to stay away from him."

"Why?" Jade asked a little worried and confused.

Suddenly Lingwood appeared alongside us.

"Can I steal Eleni for a moment," he asked.

"*You* can do whatever *you* like," Stephanie flirted as she fluttered her long black seductive eyelashes at him.

He smirked and walked over to a separate table, and like a stupid pathetic lapdog, I followed.

"Please, take a seat," he insisted.

I sat down cautiously and he was smiling his Hollywood-grin. It was hard to imagine how someone could look so perfect. Was he even real?

"Thank you for agreeing to go to the dance with me," he said very politely.

"Why the sudden change of heart?" I replied rather bluntly, as I still weren't completely sure this wasn't some sort of wind up.

"I told you. I gave up," he shrugged. His eyes were serious but that lush smile still beamed from ear to ear.

"Gave up?" I repeated in puzzlement.

"Yep, I'm done," he sighed, the smile finally fading.

"Done?" I repeated his words again with confusion.

"I'm done trying to be good. I'm done trying to stay away from you. It's not in my nature to be good," a hard edge crept into his voice and his smile had completely vanished now.

"I'm lost?" I frowned with bewilderment, "Why are you done being good? And why would you want to stay away from me? I don't understand what I have done wrong?"

That breathtaking smile reappeared, "You've done nothing wrong," he reassured me.

"Then why all this bullshit?" I moaned.

"Because I'm not a good friend to have, trust me," he smiled, but I could see behind that charming crooked smirk that the warning was real.

"Why?" I demanded impatiently.

"Because I'm not a good person. I'm the bad guy!"

"I don't agree," I challenged. "A stupid guy perhaps, but certainly not bad."

He smirked, "But you don't know me."

"No, you're right, I don't *know* you. You've made that pretty hard to achieve by avoiding me," I said frostily as my eyes narrowed.

"You have quite the temper don't you?" He snorted.

His smug face I wanted to punch right now.

"I don't like smug overconfident guys that think just because they're good-looking that they can play games and toy with people!" I snarled.

He seemed very amused as he beamed his crooked smile at me. His mood suddenly shifted as his eyes turned brooding, "You think I'm good-looking?"

I had to look away from the intensity of his stare.

"That's what you took from that?" I groaned with despair, "It wasn't meant as a compliment!"

"You know you're very attractive when you're angry," he said playfully with a cheeky smile.

I rolled my eyes and couldn't help but smile back, despite my best efforts not to. I was so frustrated that my anger was seeping away like water down a plug. How does he do that?

"So, are you not grabbing any lunch today?" I quickly said in panic to get him off the subject of me.

"No, I've been *too* distracted this lunch break to think about food," he flirted.

My jaw almost dropped but I stopped it.

"What about you?" He asked.

"I'm not hungry," I gulped. If truth be told I was a little peckish, but my stomach was so full with butterflies at that moment, that there was no way I could fit food in there, but I wasn't going to tell him that.

"Are you ok?" He asked, "You look a little flushed."

"I'm fine!" I blushed, "I have to go."

"Bye," he said with that same mischievous crooked smile.

"Bye," I replied quickly as I rushed to catch up with the girls.

"*Oh . . . my . . . god*, he is *so* into you," Stephanie giggled excitedly as we walked out of the Cafeteria.

"Careful with that one," Sofia warned for the umpteenth time.

"What's that noise?" Dotty asked.

"That's a . . ." Stephanie paused, staring. "Nice car!" She drooled.

"Wow," Jade gasped.

"That's a 66 GT 350 Mustang," I was shocked that I remembered.

"Ooooo, check you out, car expert," Stephanie scoffed.

"I know why *she* knows," Sofia said with a smirk.

"Why?" Dotty asked innocently, and we all giggled.

The sleek blood-red mustang purred through the courtyard, moving lazily as though it were some predator stalking its prey.

When its rumbling engine roared to a stop, the group of us stood in our tracks to catch a glimpse. The lean muscled man stepped out and I could have sworn I saw it in slow motion.

Linx was in a tight black T-shirt showing off his aw-so-perfect-figure that made me salivate. Faded jeans that were so tight they looked as though they needed peeling off, and I bit my lip as I thought about them being peeled off. His hair was thick and wavy, matching his dusty-black-grey leather jacket that was flung coolly over his shoulder.

"Oh . . . my . . . god," Stephanie whispered.

"You can say that again," breathed Jade.

I finally let my own breath out, "Hi Linx," I exhaled as he breezed past.

"Hey!" He replied with a smile as he walked into the cafeteria.

"*Hi . . . Linx,*" Sofia teased in a mocking voice, "You've got it bad," she giggled.

"Save some for the rest of us!" Jade joked.

"Uh-oh. Stephanie has that look in her eye, the hunting look," Dotty snorted.

"Short-dark-and-handsome had better be careful," Sofia cackled.

"He's not short. He's *perfect*!" I said in a silly lustful voice. Estella rolled her eyes and chuckled.

"You've already got Lingwood sniffing around you. What more do you want?" Stephanie complained.

"Perhaps she's after a threesome," Sofia snickered.

"Ohhhhhh that would be Heaven," Stephanie drooled, and the group all dissolved into laughter as we peered through the window at him. Dotty had strolled on ahead with Estella.

"Nice rear view," Stephanie dribbled as she checked out his butt.

"Come on lets go," Sofia finally moaned, taking in a good eyeful first, before she finally unstuck her glued eyes and dragged me and Jade away. Stephanie eventually caught us up too after she had finished her gawking.

"So, if you had the choice, Lingwood or Linx?" Estella asked with a mischievous grin.

"Eleni does have the choice by the looks of it," Stephanie chuckled, but I could sense the envy in her voice, perhaps a touch of jealousy too.

"Do they have any sisters?" Dotty sniggered.

We all laughed in response.

"I'm serious!" She chuckled.

"I'd have Linx, all day long," Jade blurted. "Lingwood *is* gorgeous, but if I had the choice," she poked her tongue through her teeth. "What about you?"

"After seeing that firm rear, I'm leaning towards Linx," Estella chuckled, "But I'd be lying if I said it wasn't a close one."

"A close one? I thought you told me to stay clear of Lingwood though?" I frowned.

"I did. But hey! A girl can fantasize," she snickered.

"I can't choose," Stephanie snorted.

"You mean you're not fussy," Sofia gibed.

"I have been known to show a man a good time if he treats me right," Stephanie replied with a smile.

"But you'd rather they treat you wrong," Sofia said with a giggle and a wink.

We all laughed.

"What about you then Sofia, who would *you* have if you had the choice?" Stephanie blurted.

"Neither!" She grumbled.

"Liar, I saw you checking out Linx's butt with the rest of us," Stephanie cackled.

"Lingwood, if he wasn't such a monster," Sofia mumbled.

"Didn't see that one coming," Jade giggled and my chin almost hit the floor too.

"Why is he a monster?" I asked.

"Animal attacks yeah. You dumb bitches really think those attacks are animals? Look at him and his creepy father, they're freaking Vampires!" Sofia snapped.

"Don't be so ridiculous," I laughed with Jade, but I noticed that Dotty, Stephanie, Estella and Sofia weren't laughing. Then a cold feeling came over me as I thought back to the first day I sat next to him and thought I imagined fangs and slit eyes for a second. But now I was being silly, my imagination was crawl back then due to lack of sleep, and I clearly hallucinated. I hadn't seen any signs of those slit eyes or fangs since, which confirmed to me that it was sleep deprivation that caused me to see that, something I certainly wasn't lacking nowadays – with all the Lingwood dreams I had been having lately.

"Just be careful!" Estella warned.

"Ok," I gulped as I nodded slowly and nervously. Perhaps he wasn't the hero I deserved, but the monster I craved.

"What about you then? Who would you choose Eleni?" Jade giggled.

I was speechless as I tried to imagine which one I'd choose if given the chance, and I couldn't come up with an answer.

"I don't know," was all I could muster as a response.

Right now I had more of a chance with Lingwood due to the age difference with Linx, but it was an impossible choice, and one I hoped I'd never have to make.

"Linx is better in bed," Stacy said as she appeared in the doorway and shoulder-barged past me.

"You've been with both?" I gasped, trying to hide the shock, sadness and jealousy . . . possibly envy.

Stacy turned, winked at me, and then strutted off.

"She's just messing with your head," Sofia growled. "In-fact I've had enough of her remarks!" Sofia ran after Stacy.

"Oh god!" We all gasped as we ran after Sofia.

"What's your problem?" Sofia snarled to Stacy.

"Your shiny bald head hurts my eyes," Stacy smirked mockingly as she stood in front of a tiny haystack.

Next thing all I saw was Stacy's faultless smooth legs shoot up into the air as her perfect-shaped foot slid out of one of her lovely red heels. The gorgeous blonde had somersaulted backwards over the haystack, the impact sending that red heel as if someone had thrown it, as it shot across the courtyard, skidding to a halt near some horse poo. If only it had gone a little bit further and landed in it! I thought with frustration as I hoped that the stony gravel scratched it up. Sofia had punched Stacy straight in the face which had caused the blonde to fall backwards over the stack, crashing to the floor in a heap, screaming and holding her jaw.

"Come on Sofia, she's not worth it," we all said as we pulled her away . . . But none of us had seen Stacy climb to her feet. She slipped off her other heel and held the tip of the shoe in her hand. I glanced back at the last minute.

"LOOK OUT!" I screamed as I shoved Sofia out of the way of the sharp high-heel . . .

Next thing I know I woke up in Linx's arms, he was carrying me to the nurse's room.

"Wha . . . what happened?" I whispered in a weak voice.

"You had a high-heel smash into the side of your head. It knocked you out. One of your friends came and got me, and now I am carrying you to the nurse's room to get checked out," he explained.

"Put me down!" I begged.

"You look awful," he told me, grinning, ignoring my protests to be put down.

The rocking of his walk wasn't helping my dizziness. He held me away from his body, scooped up in his strong biceps that supported my entire bodyweight impressively.

"You're so strong," I mumbled pathetically as I drifted in and out of consciousness.

"This is like déjà vu," he mumbled.

"What?" I said as I tried not to drift.

"Nothing," his face looked anxious as if he had let something slip, but my head hurt too much right now to ponder.

I don't know how he opened the medical room door whilst carrying me, but suddenly it was warmer so I knew we were inside.

"What have we here?" A woman's voice spoke.

I recognised the soft sweet tone, but my head was still spinning and I had firmly shut my eyes and clamped my lips in a desperate attempt to hold back the nausea. He gently placed me down onto the crackly paper that covered the awful rock hard slim bed. I opened my eyes to see an angel peering down at me. Soon I realised that it wasn't an angel, but the next best thing. A goddess of pure natural beauty. Waves of silver and hues of a blushing sky tinted the length of hair that cascaded down to frame a delicate face. I wanted to reach out and stroke the stunning hair that was winter wrapped around spring like a violet morning, as though feathers had been dipped in amaranthine ink. It seemed to change slightly depending which light you caught it in, cascading mystical waves of sunrise with pale pastels in the hues of abalone. Sometimes it even looked a dusty-grey violet, or a waterfall capturing sunset. However I saw it, the quicksilver-blue cascade of her unicorn lilac pastels and mystical silky mane, was something you could get lost in forever.

Her skin reminded me of whipped- milk and her autumn burnt-red lips were mouth-watering-beautiful. Indira was a phenomenon that I could study for hours, perhaps days. Forget Lingwood and Linx, if I had the choice it would be her! I was horrified by that thought. I wasn't a lesbian, but I was so attracted to her. Although this time it was *her* studying me. Looking down on me with the iciest-blue eyes I have ever seen. Glaring back up into those heavenly eyes, I was like a deer caught in headlights; it was like looking into a snow-blizzard.

"Your head is bruised and slightly cut," her soft lullaby voice soaked gorgeously into my ear canals, as she placed her smooth hands through my hair.

"She got hit with a shoe," Linx chuckled slightly as he said it.

"We will need to talk about that sword that called out to you Eleni," she suggested, there seemed to be a hint of lavender swirling in her snow-blizzard eyes now, which made her even more mystifyingly beautiful.

I tried to nod but my head hurt too much.

"I'll come and find you next week and we can talk privately," Indira's soothing voice promised.

I tingled slightly at the thought of talking with her alone. Imagining being by-myself with such a goddess raised my heart-rate and excitement.

"Lay still, I am going to heal you," Indira's perfect voice reassured.

I did as she said and she placed her palms onto my head. A sense of calmness came over me. I noticed Indira's lip curl slightly as if she felt some sort of pain. She then stepped back from me.

"All is well now child," she comforted.

"Thank you," I said, amazed, as I placed my hand to the back of my head. The cut and bruise were gone. "How?" I mumbled.

"Thank you," Linx said to her as he walked towards me. "Lets go," he insisted to me.

I noticed that Indira had sat down. She looked a little uncomfortable.

"Is she ok?" I asked as Linx ushered me through the door.

"She took your pain," he said.

"I know. It is gone. But is she ok?" I asked again.

"No, *she . . . took . . . your . . . pain,*" he enunciated every syllable, as if he were talking to someone mentally handicapped.

"Took it where?" I was being blonde now and I knew it, even though I wasn't blonde.

He sighed and rolled his eyes.

"Any pain you had and any injuries, she now has them instead of you," he explained.

My face twitched and dropped with shock.

"That's terrible," I gasped.

"I know, but it is what she does. She's a healer like your father," Linx pointed out.

I instantly thought back to something Dotty had said to me ages ago about the headmaster healing Sofia from her cancer. Suddenly it all came blurting out of my mouth uncontrollably, "Does dad have cancer?"

"What?" Linx raised an eyebrow, flabbergasted by the randomness of my question.

"Dotty told me that Sofia had cancer and that the headmaster healed her," I elaborated.

"Your father is a very resourceful and powerful Sorcerer-wizard. He has manipulated the elements for decades," Linx replied.

"You didn't answer my question!" I persisted.

Linx slowly nodded and my mouth gaped with disbelief.

"Will he die?" I gulped.

"The stones keep him alive and powerful. It is the Stones that keep the magic from dying out on Earth. That is why a Stone Chasers job is so important," Linx clarified.

"What will happen if they run out? Where are these stones?" My voice quickened and almost squeaked as my anxiety took over.

"They can only be located near the gates of Hell, deep within the mountain. The deeper you go, then the more you'll find, but the deeper you go the more demons attack. I've lost so many Stone Chasers over the years and because the swords power chooses its master or mistress, it means there is no guarantee that the ones who die will be replaced. I was so relieved when the stone chaser sword picked you. As we are very few these days and if we get wiped out, then the magic gets wiped out, and the demons will breach the walls and escape, destroying the world."

"And Lucifer?" I gulped.

"No. Lucifer's cage was sealed by Reverend Crone and The Angels. It can't ever be opened. But trust me; Demons are just as scary and probably even crueller, twisted and sinister. They certainly know how to scare and cause mayhem."

"Yep! Demons are pretty scary," I shivered, "But I don't believe for a second that they're worse than the Devil," I said sceptically.

"Well, according to Reverend Crone. All Angels are good. Including Lucifer, they just believe different things. Lucifer hates mankind because they are corrupt and pollute the beautiful planet that his father - *God*, created. And he feels let down that his father forgives them so easily. So, Lucifer created Hell and then created Demons to drag corrupted souls down there, as he didn't want God forgiving them and allowing them into Heaven. He originally wanted to wipe out all mankind, but decided he couldn't hurt his father like that. So, in the end he just wanted to punish the bad, agreeing to leave good souls untouched to go to Heaven. The problem was that the Demons he created to drag the bad humans to Hell, turned out even worse than the humans and only corrupted mankind more. Lucifer had good intentions but they backfired on him. So, Lucifer begged God for forgiveness. Understanding that creation wasn't as easy as he thought, so he cut his father some slack, promising to wipe out the demons that he had created. God forgave as he always does, and sent Lucifer and Michael to lead an army of Angels to rid the world of Demons. They teamed up with Holy-men and killed the demons before the monsters had the chance to slaughter the human race. But Michael then discovered that his brother Lucifer was secretly recruiting Angels to help return the world to its former glory, - untainted by humanity. Lucifer knew that Demons were making Humans even worse. So he decided it would be a lot easier to rid the entire world of everything, rather than to keep exhaustingly trying to separate the good from the bad. God decided to stay out of it and didn't want to know - he eventually gave up caring for the bickering of his children. So, Michael took matters into his own hands and led an army of Angels to arrest Lucifer to stand trial in Heaven for his crimes. But Lucifer fought back with an army of freshly made demons and a couple of hundred Angels that he had managed to convince to join his cause. A great battle commenced and Lucifer lost. They sealed him in his cage and that was the end of that. So, Reverend Crone says that Lucifer only wanted to save the planet from mankind's corruption and destruction and couldn't understand God's forgiveness. But it soon became clear that God created the sandbox but he didn't care who played in it and how rough they played. So, I think the moral of the story is, God doesn't like confrontation and just wants creation to thrive, and will always forgive, and Lucifer doesn't want to see things destroyed and wants some sort of order and punishment. Therefore both the intentions are good, depending on which point of view you take," Linx explained.

"Wow, that was deep. Thanks for that *story,*" I yawned teasingly.

Linx frowned and playfully punched my arm.

I giggled.

"Reverend Crone told a different story to us," I then said.

"Oh really?" Linx seemed curious.

"He said that Lucifer wanted to destroy everything that God made in order to get back at his father for not caring and for creating good and evil for his own entertainment."

"Well yes, that is now true, but originally Lucifer only wanted to rid the world of mankind and the demons he had created. Now after sitting in his cage for thousands of years, he's become even more bitter and twisted than ever," Linx explained.

"How could you know that?" I asked.

"You know that glass globe that you used to see Master Bob in the past?" He said.

I nodded slowly.

"Well, Reverend Crone can use that same globe to read the thoughts of people nearby. He used it not so long ago to see what Lucifer was thinking, and that was it. He has gone from wanting to save the world from mankind to literally wanting to destroy everything his father created, to get back at him!" Linx explained.

"Oh ok, I get it now," I said with a nod, "So the power of prayer, is it all bullshit? Should I even bother preying to God?"

"The short version is that God created the sandbox and doesn't care how rough we all play. The long version, from what I understand from the oldest Holy-man in the world - Reverend Crone, is that God is complicated. God is neither bad nor good. He forgives everything. Now, is that because he doesn't care? Or is it because he is really nice and forgiving? It all depends on your point of view on *that* one. One thing for certain though, is God prefers to let the chips fall where they may. God likes to allow events to happen without changing them. So, he may or may not answer your prayer, but it is always worth keeping faith and preying. He has been known to answer from time to time on the very rare occasion. Although if you think of the billions that prey all the time to him, he can't answer them all," he explained.

"I think I get it now. A bit like the film *'Bruce Almighty'* when *'Morgan Freeman'* explains to *'Jim Carrey'* how difficult it is to help everyone?" I said.

He rolled his eyes.

"Exactly!" He sighed, "Come on, let's get you back to your class, your friends are probably worried."

I nodded and we walked back to my next class.

"To change the subject, you scared me for a minute back there when I saw you unconscious," he admitted as we walked. His tone sounded as though he was confessing to a humiliating weakness.

"Awww. You're cute," I replied sweetly.

He snorted and then turned to me.

"Seriously, be careful. Stacy can be a spiteful bitch," he warned.

"Were you and her, a . . ." I paused, not sure how to say the words, or if it was any of my actual business.

"A what?" He frowned with a smirk as confusion shot across his handsome face.

We had made it to the entrance of my classroom now.

I smiled awkwardly.

"Never mind," I sighed, feeling a little embarrassed as I rushed into the classroom and Linx followed me in.

"She's had a little bump on the head but she's got the all clear from the nurse," he explained to my teacher.

I could see Lingwood glaring at Linx from across the classroom. Linx then turned and smiled at him, before turning and smiling at me.

"See you after school for training," he said to me with a nod, and then he walked out.

Lingwood stared at me with those intense eyes throughout the class, totally distracting me. I couldn't help but send a few seductive smiles back his way. But made sure I didn't get too carried away.

"Oh my god I was so worried about you," Sofia said after class had finished as she gripped me in a tight hug. I gently placed my hands around her and hugged back, feeling a little bewildered by her behaviour. Sofia wasn't one for small-talk, girlie chats, and especially hugs. Usually.

"Are you ok?" I frowned as I looked her in the face.

"Of course I am," she sounded a little defensive. "Can't I be worried for a friend?"

"Of course you can," I smiled. "What actually happened?"

"Stacy tried to attack me with her heel, and you stupidly put your head in the way," Sofia snickered.

"Oh, I know, remind me not to do *that* again," I sighed as I rubbed my head.

Lingwood then approached.

"I think Linx absolutely loathes me," he laughed.

"Yeah . . . *She's* fine, thanks for asking! A little less testosterone and dick-measuring," Sofia grumbled as she shoulder-barged past him.

"Ouch!" Lingwood sniggered as he looked back at her.

Sofia glanced over her shoulder with a glare that could burn through lead as she turned the corner and out of sight. It was hard to believe that she admitted to us that she fancied him earlier. It was hard to believe that she liked anyone, but now I knew her toughness was an act; she gave herself away when she hugged me just now. Something in her eyes said that she was so relieved that I was alright.

"I think she loathes you too," I giggled.

"Oh, I dunno about that. It's all part of my charm," he said cheerfully with a wink as he smiled at me, "How are you feeling?"

"I'm fine. Thank god Linx scooped me up and took me to the nurse," I said and watched his reaction.

His eye twitched slightly.

"I'll have to thank him for that," he said calmly.

"You know, I doubt Linx loathes you," I said, feeling a little guilty at trying to make him jealous. That wasn't kind, but I wanted to see his reaction, like a test.

"Yeah, he does loath me, I've seen his face," he chuckled.

"You don't know that," I argued.

Suddenly, Stephanie, Dotty, Jade and Estella appeared in the corridor. Sofia had gone and got them and there were a lot of girlie screeches as they ran up to me, hugging me tight.

"So glad you are ok," they all said.

"I'm fine," I sighed.

"Thank god Linx showed up," Jade said and I saw Lingwood roll his eyes.

"I saw you from a distance, why didn't you help?" Stephanie asked as she shot a frowning glare Lingwoods way.

"You saw?" I gasped.

Lingwood nodded.

"Then why didn't you come to her rescue?" Stephanie grumbled.

"I'm not good around blood," he said awkwardly, "And I saw that Linx was there. I figured the last thing you needed was testosterone and dick-measuring between us," he glanced at Sofia with a smirk as he said it. "I trusted him to keep you safe for me," he reassured as he threw his arm around my shoulder giving me a squeeze.

"What a saint," Sofia mumbled with a frown.

"I'm sorry, have I done something to upset you?" Lingwood's tone was cutting as he turned, glaring right into Sofia's eyes.

I could see that this took her by surprise, even if she hid it well.

"I'm just protective over my friends," she said, never breaking eye-contact with his intense glare, something that I struggled to do.

"If you don't like the sight of blood, then I suggest you don't hurt my friend," she warned.

Lingwood smiled, completely unfazed by her threat.

"She's lucky to have such a passionate friend. I won't hurt her," he reassured.

Sofia's expression softened as she desperately tried to keep up her frowning bitch-face.

"Good," she grumbled, turning away sharply. "Come on lets go, we have potion class," she said to the group, trying not to look at Lingwood as she said it.

"All part of my charm," he whispered to me with a cheeky crooked smile.

I smirked and looked away before Sofia saw me. If he could charm *her* into submission, then what chance did my defence have?

"Are you coming?" Dotty asked.

"Oh no, potion smoke makes me feel dizzy at the best of times. It's the last place I want to be," I groaned.

"The teacher will pulse you if you miss it," Jade cautioned.

"I can take care of that," Lingwood whispered.

"How?" I asked.

"Mrs Connolly is a friend of my father, I'll talk to her and say that due to you sustaining a head injury and feeling a bit dizzy, the last thing you feel like is breathing in potion fumes. She'll understand," he said with a smile as he strolled on ahead of us.

"Hmmm. Maybe I *would,* choose Lingwood over Linx," Stephanie pondered and everyone groaned in despair as we all rolled our eyes and stalked close behind.

"You shouldn't be so harsh on him," I lashed out at Sofia.

"His father is a monster, and I'm still undecided on if he's following in that man's footsteps," Sofia retaliated.

"Well, you could be a bit friendlier," I moaned.

"Yeah well, my niceness has to be earned. I don't trust him!"
She grumbled.

"He seems ok to me," Stephanie whispered with a giggle.

"You think all male-species are nice," Estella jumped in.

"True," Stephanie shrugged, "But *this ones* especially nice."

"Just be careful," Sofia pleaded.

"Yeah, take precautions . . . You know," Stephanie said as she
slipped her finger inside her fist.

"Ewwwwwww!" I screeched in horror.

"Not everyone gives that up as easy as you," Jade giggled.

Stephanie rolled her eyes, "I'm just trying to give advice. If you
don't want it, fine by me," she stomped off.

"Wait," we all called out, but Stephanie continued walking.

"I'll go and calm Dramageddon down. See you lot later on,"
Estella moaned as she chased after Stephanie.

"I was only joking," Jade moped.

"Stephanie's fine. She's thick-skinned and too unintelligent to
realise when someone is being mean. Her real upset isn't *you*
Jade, it's jealousy over the attention that Eleni is getting from
two good-looking lads. She'll get over it once she hops on some
other poor boy. She's probably having withdrawal symptoms
because she's gone a day without sex," Sofia said bluntly.

"Ouch!" I gasped. "Remind me not to get on the wrong side of
you."

Sofia shrugged, "I like Stephanie. Her hearts in the right place,
but she was born with a male brain, if you know what I mean. I

don't judge her, but I also don't beat around the bush with my truth."

"We've noticed," Jade snorted.

"Whatever," Sofia groaned as we finally got to the classroom door.

Lingwood appeared in the doorway.

"It's all sorted," he said as he flashed his incredible teeth.

I glanced over his shoulder and the teacher nodded with a smile.

"Wow," I mumbled, "Thanks."

"See you later," Jade, Dotty, and Sofia said to us with a disappointed tone and envy in their eyes as they went and sat in the classroom.

We strolled down the corridor and headed outside and I was so relieved that my wrist wasn't pulsing as Lingwood held the door open for me like a gentleman.

"We live in a world where women can open doors on there own, ya know," I said playfully.

"Are you a feminist?" He asked seriously.

I shrugged, "I dunno. If truth be told I'm not entirely sure I even know what it means."

"Really?" He smirked. "Let's you and I go and sit on that bench and I'll explain it to you."

"Sure," I mumbled, preoccupied by the way he'd said 'You and I.' I liked it way more than I really should have.

We strolled over and sat down on the wooden bench and I felt a nice calm breeze gently brush against my face.

His voice was like melted syrup and his eyes were overwhelming. "There are thousands of people who feel we've already arrived at equality for men and women," his soft voice paused for a second with a grin and I smiled back as he continued. "There are also thousands of people who believe we're not at all there yet, and support continuing efforts to pave the way for equal rights for men and women. Feminism at its core is about equality of men and women, not 'sameness.' So many people offer up the argument that women are not the 'same' as men so there can't be equality. In other words, because their bodies are different, perhaps weaker and smaller, and because men and women have different physical capabilities, these physical differences mean equality is not possible. It's critical to understand that 'same' does not mean 'equal.' The issue here is about equal rights and equal access to opportunities. Men and women don't have to be the 'same' in physicality to have the right to equality. I'd love to see that argument that women and men aren't the same so they can't be equal, disappear forever. In my view, it's a misguided one . . . Am I boring you yet?" He laughed.

I shook my head quickly and smiled contently at him, I found it incredibly cute how he worded things so carefully and in such great-detail to explain it to me.

"Please continue. I find it fascinating," I said kindly, but if truth be said, Lingwood could be droning on about dog-poo and my ears would still enjoy his voice. I studied his lips as he carried on speaking.

"There are thousands who believe in equal rights but find *feminism* a word and a movement that doesn't align with their personal beliefs or values. It's abundantly clear that our specific views on these issues are rooted deeply in our own personal and direct experiences, rather than on any data, research, or science surrounding the issues. In other words, if we've personally faced discrimination, we know beyond doubt that it exists. But if we haven't faced it ourselves, we often doubt that it happens. Both conscious and unconscious gender bias is rampant within us, but most of us aren't even aware of it. There is a great divide among men and women, and among the people of the world who see things dramatically differently from each other."

I studied his lips. He had a mouth that could keep you up at night. The upper lip was beautifully sculpted, a little sensitive, a whole lot sensual . . . I suddenly realised he had stopped speaking.

"But women are different from men, that's why we are attracted to each other," I challenged and without realising fluttered my eyelashes at him.

The sexual and kissable lips begun to move again, "Gay people would argue that that isn't necessarily true, Eleni," he argued.

"Feelings are feelings, regardless of if you are different or not. But you're right," he admitted but with a smug smirk, "We are different, but that doesn't mean we shouldn't be equal. If there were two young boys in a classroom, and one was physically weaker and smaller than the other, would we believe it's right to keep the weaker, smaller boy from having the same access to the teacher, to learning, to the computers, to the books and class resources, to other children in the class because he didn't have the same physical strength as the other boy?"

"You're right," I gasped, trying to keep up as my own voice inside my head begun to describe him to me. *His long dark hair trickled down his back and around his face, framing features so fine that they could have easily of been a picture of an old Roman coin or medallion. High cheekbones and a classical straight nose, and those lush lips* . . . were moving again!

"A lot of people hate feminists because it is associated with women who hate men and everything men stand for," he explained, "But these women give the true meaning a bad name . . . Feminism at its core is supposed to be about choice. Feminists can wear whatever they want. If you cannot choose freely how to behave, speak, act and present yourself, then you're moving backwards. And if I'm honest I feel the same about Meninists."

"Meninists?" I giggled. "What's that?"

"It's a word I've made up to counter Feminists," he chuckled. "People take terms *too* literately. Women should have the freedom to do whatever they want, and so should men. Meninists and Feminists just doing whatever they feel like doing, knowing that ones behaviours don't reflect on the others. No judgment. Women and men should be partners in everything, but everything needs to be their own choices. Sadly, some individuals think that that means men should stop being men and treat women as though they were also men, - and if a man doesn't, then he is a sexist or a male-chauvinist, and if a woman lets him then she's pathetic. Basically, what I'm getting at is, if I as a man want to open a door for a pretty girl, then I will, and that doesn't make me a sexist chauvinist, or means that I am taking away your right as a free independent woman. I do because I want to do, and that's the way the world should be. If a woman takes me opening a door as me taking away her freedom instead of a compliment, the same way a man that get's intimidated by a woman being too forward and independent, instead of feeling chuffed about it, reflects more on them and their own insecurities than anything else," he smiled. "Are you following?"

"I think so," I mumbled. *Are his eyes black or red? Or both? –* I pondered as I tried desperately to listen to his trickling honey voice that drizzled into my ears, and not to keep getting distracted by his incredible good-looks.

"Ok, let me try and simplify it," he said as he paused for thought. "I opened the door because I wanted to, but I'd be equally as fine if you opened the door yourself, and you should be happy with having the door opened for you, and equally as happy if I didn't open the door for you, but you shouldn't expect me to open the door for you and I shouldn't expect you to let me open the door for you. Basically, equality should just be for work, money and expectations. With the exception to a working environment being equal, nobody should expect anything from anyone and that's equality. People do because they want to do, not because they are expected to. A man should not expect a woman to be all giggly and feminine and to behave in a certain way, and women shouldn't expect the same from men. But when it comes to work and money, we should expect to be treated equally. Understand? - I think I'll stop now," he laughed.

"I think I got it," I sniggered as I pretended to yarn.

"Did I bore you? I'm sorry," he said seriously.

"Oh, god . . . No! . . . You could never bore me," I backpedalled. Suddenly his heavenly smile went from ear to ear and I realised he was messing with me.

"You git!" I playfully slapped his arm.

He laughed and it was a beautiful chuckle that gave the same relaxing feeling to your mind and ears that Classical Music does.

"You know, you should totally come to 'The Grey-Beach Water Resort' this weekend. Stephanie arranged it, and there are a few of us going," I said.

Then disappointment coursed through me.

"I'm out of town this weekend."

"Oh," I replied. "No worries."

"Have fun at the beach, and try not to drown," he chuckled.

"I'll do my best," I smirked. "Won't I see you tomorrow?"

"No, I'm starting my weekend early."

"You're bunking class?" I gasped.

He turned and smiled at me. "You should try it sometime."

"I would but I don't like the wrist pain that that stupid pulsing gives me," I replied, although if truth be told, even without the wrist pulsing, I was too much of a coward to bunk off.

The bell chimed loudly.

"You'd better be off," he turned, looking me directly in the face, utilizing the full power of his burning reddish-black eyes. I nodded helplessly, paralysed by their magnetic pull.

"Wouldn't want to keep Linx waiting," he chuckled as he got up off the bench, a hint of sarcasm mixed with bitterness in his tone.

"Would you like a pint of bitter with that jealously?" I joked.

"See you Monday," he promised as he strolled off, ignoring my dig.

"Have a good weekend," I shouted out to him.

He turned and nodded, then disappeared through a door.

I was once again distracted when training with Linx, and I blamed it on my head injury, although it wasn't the injury, it was Lingwood and that intoxicating glare that stayed on my mind, but I couldn't tell Linx that. He understood that I wasn't quite with it due to the injury and he let me off lightly. I was momentarily distracted by his dashing body and boyish charm, as he walked me back to my dorm room.

"What did you try and ask me earlier?" He locked his green-blue eyes upon me and I tensed.

"Err," I played dumb as I was completely caught off guard.

"Stacy," he reminded me.

I swallowed hard as I now knew I was being backed into a corner and had to come clean.

"I just wanted to know if you two have ever dated or been together," I blurted.

"Oh," he gasped.

"Not that it's any of my business, which is why I didn't ask you in the end. It's only because Stacy bragged about sleeping with you and Lingwood, to us girls . . . No idea why she came out with it, we weren't even talking about you," I tried to sound convincing. "I'm really not *that* bothered and I don't even know why I asked it and I kinda wish I hadn't of mentioned it, as you've now forced me to ask you and I am embarrassed and, and . . ."

He stopped me.

"Its ok, Little E," he reassured me with a chuckle, allowing me to finally stop for breath. I didn't need a mirror to tell me that I had gone redder than a tomato. "She was a mistake. A mistake I'm sure many guys before – and, after me, have made," he opened up.

I felt a rush of jealousy shoot through me and I hoped my poker face stayed strong. "And Lingwood rejected her," he continued. "At least that's the rumour. The only guy ever to say no to her charms, apparently. But believe me if I could go back in time then I would have rejected her too. She's not a nice person Eleni," he explained truthfully and I felt that jealousy seep away at his refreshing honesty.

"What happened between you two?" I found myself asking as I sensed the sadness in his voice. "Did she break your heart?"

"I finished it with her," he mumbled. "I'm all for going with the flow and seeing where things end up," he paused and winked, trying to act cool like boys do, then he carried on, "But I realised she wasn't relationship material and I wanted more than just good-looks, I wanted a life-partner," he said passionately and I almost melted at the cuteness.

"Man up!" Sofia snorted as she breezed past us and into the dorm room.

"Love you too sweetheart," he called out to her.

She swung round and with a playful smile on her face, stuck her middle-finger up at him as she slammed the door. He laughed, and turned back towards me.

"Anyway," he said awkwardly, "Chick-flick-moment-over," he winked at me again with a charming smile before walking off.

"Hey!" I called out to him as I ran and caught him up. "I'm always here for you if you need to let off steam," I reassured him. I hated that stereotype that men need to keep their feelings inside.

"Yeah I think I'm ok, thanks," he said coolly, "I'm not going to lose no sleep over a girl"

Clearly he was backpedalling now, regretting the momentary slip up of letting his feelings loose, and trying to act like he didn't care. I smirked as I found it so cute.

"I'm here for you," I reassured with a smile as I gave him a playful punch on the arm, "You big softy."

"Oh I'm not all soft," he flirted, another slip up of feelings he hadn't intended on showing me.

"Oh really?" I said with intriguing eyes and a mischievous smile.

His eyes bulged and he choked slightly before saying, "I really have to go."

I nodded, trying not to laugh at his blushing.

"Bye," I said as I walked off in the opposite direction grinning like a Cheshire cat.

When I got to my dorm, all the girls were sitting on the sofa and chairs excited for my long awaited arrival. Sofia, Stephanie, Dotty, Estella, and even Jade was there. They were hoping for some juicy-details of my bunking off lesion with heart-throb-Lingwood, and found themselves bitterly disappointed when I informed them that we had spent the hour talking about feminism.

"You mean you haven't even got to first base with *any* of them? You've spent all this time with Linx *and* Lingwood, and you haven't even kissed one of them?" Stephanie seemed horrified.

"Not everyone moves through the bases like a baseball player Stephanie!" Sofia snickered and Stephanie frowned.

"I'm going to go to bed," I said with a yawn, and I left them all giggling and gossiping. I would have usually stayed and talked, but I couldn't wait to get to sleep so I could see Lingwood in my dreams.

3- BUYING TIME

Jealousaw's mammoth spacecraft known as 'The Death Stalker' occupied a position of deadly prominence in the Imperial Ice-fleet. The sleekly elongated ship was possibly the largest existing ship in the Galaxy. It had certainly proved the most dreaded and most devastating warship of its time. Amongst the airshafts on this huge and monstrous spacecraft which still loomed above the only entrance into Earth - the wormhole that lead to Stadley Hold, Lukamore scavenged. He had hidden and had survived for nearly two months now, on eating spiders, cooking mutant-space-rats with his fire-blade, and drinking the condensation that built up in the air ducts. His muscle-mass had decreased rapidly and his strength was almost non-existent due to this diet . . . But he was alive, even if it was barely. The Dark Lord often taunted him, speaking to him inside his own mind. *You can't hide forever Lukamore.* The terrifying deep voice would repeat over and over. *I will find you eventually. There is no escape!*

Lukamore had sabotaged the ships electronics which disabled their power. Despite the Space-station-defence being wiped out, which weakened the shield that kept the wormhole safe from being entered, Jealousaw's own ship hadn't the energy-resources to take advantage of that, thanks to Lukamore.

Absolute assurance reigned in the heart of every crew member aboard this impressive vessel. Confidence and arrogance beyond belief was installed in every soldier and officer. But something also burned within their souls. Terror – Terror of merely the sound of the familiar heavy footsteps as they echoed through the colossal ship. Crew members dreaded these footfalls and shuddered whenever they were heard approaching. The heavy stomps of impatience would thud along with the eerie rhythmic mechanical human breathing, like a scuba tank regulator. Followed by the infamous chesty-wheezy cough and throat groans, that sounded hauntingly supernatural and terrifyingly inhuman. Just the clamour of these nightmarish sounds filled everyone with anxiety, as it meant only one thing . . . Jealousaw was approaching! Towering above them in his black cloak and concealing demonic-grey mask that was hidden under the ghostly-black-hood, their much feared leader entered the main control deck, and the men around him fell silent.

Lukamore peered through a tiny vent high above them as silence smothered the room in what seemed to be an endless moment. There were no sounds except the odd bleeps from the crafts control-panels and of course the chilling slow wheezes that came from Jealousaw. The ebony figure of the dark lord glared out of the huge window at the swirling wormhole that he could not enter.

"Admiral Piett," Jealousaws voice boomed as he twisted sharply towards him.

"Yes my lord," the grey-haired man with a stern face gulped nervously as he looked up across the wide bridge at the dark figure approaching him fast.

"Are you making progress with the power repairs?" His terrifying deep voice that was distorted by the demonic breathing mask asked, as he peered down the steps towards him.

The Admiral gazed up respectfully to Jealousaw, who loomed above him like a black-robed all-powerful and supreme god.

"Yes, sir," the Admirals voice breathed slowly as he chose his words with extreme caution. The Dark Lord has been known to snap many necks - Captains, Generals, and Admirals, with just the power of his mind over the years, all because they failed to impress him in some way. "The Shields will be back up within a few weeks! We ha . . ."

"GOOD!" Jealousaw's deep voice interrupted abruptly, startling the Admiral, "And the progress on the ships power resources?"

The Admiral swallowed loudly before he spoke, "Maybe another month or two before we are at maximum strength, but we are working as hard as we can."

"I hope so, for *your* sake Admiral," Jealousaws threatening voice bellowed, "I've been most unimpressed by your apparent lack of progress."

The Admiral stood up a little taller, fear spread across his face.

"We will double our efforts," he promised, "But the damage we sustained from the intruders sabotage isn't easily fixed and we . . ."

"See to it personally Admiral," The Dark Lord broke in angrily, "I want full power and not excuses!"

"Yes my lord," he replied as sweat slowly dripped down his forehead.

"Don't fail me again . . . Admiral!" Jealousaws threatening voice warned with a pointed finger before he turned away and stomped out of the control-room.

The Admiral turned and puffed out his cheeks.

Lukamore smirked as he used his last bit of magical-strength, to blow up the control computer on the other side of the room. The explosion rocketed and men rushed with fire extinguishers to put out the flames.

The Admirals jaw hit the deck and he looked as though he was going to burst into tears.

"GET THOSE FIRES OUT!!!" He ordered as his eyes bulged from his head in disbelief.

"Sir," a man said as he approached.

"What is it Captain?" The Admiral snapped.

"If this computer isn't salvageable, it could set us back weeks, maybe months," the Captain exhaled with panic.

"Yes, yes, thank you Captain *Obvious!* I am well aware of our present situation," the Admiral groaned as he leaned heavily on the desk. "Any progress made with finding the intruder? *Please* give me some good news."

"We have searched and secured the east wing and south wing of the ship. We haven't yet located him, but we are closing in all around. He will be running out of places to hide soon," the Captain insisted.

"Well Jealousaw wants him found now!" The Admiral barked, "Get it done, Captain!"

"Yes sir," the Captain nodded as he turned to a man standing nearby, "General Smith, I need every available man at your disposal to carry out a full sweep of this area. That computer was sabotaged, which means he must be nearby. Find him!" The Captain ordered.

The General nodded. "Yes captain," and walked off hastily.

Lukamore knew that his life was limited and that it was only a matter of time before they found him, but as he crawled tiredly through the ventilation shafts he still couldn't help but grin. Despite his fate most probably being a torturous agonizing death at the hands of Jealousaw, he took comfort in knowing that with every destruction and every bit of chaos he caused up here, he was buying more time for those he loved down there – On Earth.

"I know that you are somewhere in the ventilation shafts Lukamore" – The demonic voice rattled his brain. – *"Destroying that computer takes a mind-power that relied on vision. The only viewpoint without being discovered would be the vents. Your eagerness has given away your position"* – The deep voice had a hint of satisfaction to its tone. Lukamore knew now that he needed to use the Fire-pulse-mines he had strapped to his belt. He had hoped to use it as a means of escape somehow, but now realised he wasn't getting out of this alive. His mission to buy time for his friends and family had now altered to a suicide mission. Now he only had one option – to make his way to the engine room and bring this ship and all its evil crew, down!

4- SCARY TALES

That Friday-buzz-feeling was in the air around school. Everyone was excited for the weekend, but at the same time nobody could quite be bothered with work today, with the attitude that it's Friday, so screw it! I hadn't been looking forward to today and it more than lived up to my non-expectations. Stephanie seemed to get a kick out of telling the damsel in distress story and how Linx had carried me to safety. A chorus of sighs and whispers seemed to follow me around the hallways and chatter would stop instantly as I walked by as though someone had thrown a switch. I wasn't sure what was going on at first, but it was obvious I was the centre of the gossip. Jade eventually told me that rumours about me and Linx had begun to spread thanks to The-Knight-In-Shining-Armour story that News-of-the-world- Stephanie had been giggling about all morning. - Thanks Stephanie!
I still found my eyes searching for Lingwood, even though I knew he wasn't in school today. I didn't even have training with Eye-candy-Linx later to look forward to, as he had been called out of the castle on important Stone-Chaser business, a teacher informed me. So this day was getting better and better by the minute!
I intercepted a few unfriendly glances from Stacy, but that was nothing new. It was difficult to frown back at her, as even when she was scowling at you, she looked so pretty. I certainly

didn't blame Linx for sleeping with her, but I was really shocked that Lingwood had turned her down. That must had been quite denting to her ego. I couldn't help a smug bitchy smirk at the thought of her getting rejected. I imagine rejection is something she certainly wouldn't be used to.

I was shocked and amazed at how malice the girls were around school towards me. The rumours of me possibly having the two best-looking-lads in school wanting to hang out with me - certainly didn't boost my own popularity. It seemed to have quite the reverse affect.

I stayed concealed in the tight-knitted-pack of Jade, Stephanie, Estella, Dotty and Sofia. I hid amongst them as much as I could throughout the day, avoiding the constant bitchiness from the jealous horde of felines that had their claws out ready to attack.

Then just to add more glory to a glorious day, I found out I had detention after school for our fight yesterday, despite my protests at the injustice and me claiming that I was the victim of a vicious attack by a high-heel and not actually involved. I still had to sit there with Sofia and Stacy. We had to write lines for an hour of why fighting is bad. Then after about three hours of that, we were given a further two hours of wrist-pulsing on full power to motivate us not to break the school rules again. I thought they only did the wrist pulse to remind you if you are late for class, but I had never experienced it on full power before. It felt like a burning sensation followed by dreadful pins and needles. The pain was borderline unbearable, and certainly uncomfortable to the point of crying almost. I was just glad I wasn't going through it alone and I felt a sort of satisfaction at seeing Stacy squirm and yelp.

I was so relieved when the extra *looooong* day finally drew to a close and detention was over, I clutched my throbbing wrist and rushed off. I had been a little excited about tomorrow's trip to 'The Grey-Beach Water Resort', but after barely surviving today in school from all the catty gossipers, and now feeling sorry for myself and my sore wrist, I was now dreading the possibility of seeing some of them at the beach tomorrow and wasn't fully sure if my wrist would recover in time. I considered faking being sick, - but I knew Stephanie wouldn't buy it, and I certainly didn't want to let the girls down.

I had meant to sleep in that morning, but typically on the days where I want to lay-in and sleep, I'd always wake early. Yet guaranteed if I needed to get up for something important like school or an event, then my body would have other ideas.

I squinted and it took more than a few blinks and eye-rubbing before my brain finally woke up and my lids became less heavy.

I noticed something was unusual in the room, and then realised why I had woken up so early. There was an odd brightness penetrating the window. Clear yellow light streamed in through the glass and I couldn't believe it. I rushed over to the window to have a look, and sure enough, there was the sun. It was strange seeing the gorgeous fiery glow and feeling its warm touch, it was as if I had woken up back on the farm in Blosoms Hill. My body had only just begun to adjust to the cold, dull, rainy and misty climate of this place, and now the heavens are unfairly teasing me with this more than rare sunshine.

Clouds hovered slightly around the horizon, but majority of the sky was a lovely navy. I lingered by the window as long as possible, afraid that if I looked away then the sapphire would vanish.

Stephanie had clearly strutted her stuff and flirted her way into getting one of the boys in class who owned a minivan, to give us a lift through town to the beach. Jade, Dotty, Estella, Sofia and I, followed her down into the courtyard. Me and Sofia both still instinctively clutched our wrists despite the pain being long gone now.

"Is this everyone?" The boy asked.

"Yes. Everyone that is riding with us. Everybody else is making their own way there," Stephanie replied, "This is Johnny, by the way."

"*Hi Johnny,*" we all said simultaneously with a giggle as we climbed into the van.

"Nice to officially meet you girls," he replied with a smirk. Stephanie of course jumped into the front seat alongside the poor helpless boy that she was going to eat alive. I almost felt sorry for him as he tried to act cool and confident. I could see the panic flare in his eyes and the sweat building on his forehead. Stephanie was like a parasite that got inside boys minds, and it didn't always bring out the best in them.

"Oh, I found out a bit of info on your mysterious boyfriend," Jade giggled.

"Boyfriend?" I said bewilderedly.

"Which one?" Stephanie sniggered from the front.

"Lingwood," said Jade, "Eleni, listen to this. He's in my spellbound class, and I sit just across from him. He's from Italy," she sighed, "And he's *so* romantic. Stephanie dropped her books, and he picked them up for her."

Sofia made a wry face, "How clumsy of Stephanie," she remarked sarcastically and sceptically.

"He's so sweet," Stephanie shouted back from the front seat.

"Yeah I bet," Estella said as she rolled her eyes.

Johnny scrunched up his face as he glanced in the mirror at us. "Lingwood Putin is a freak," he groaned.

"And why's that?" I spat back defensively.

"He's always on his own or with his dad, and that guy gives me the creeps," he replied.

"So, just because he hangs out on his own it makes him a freak, does it?" I quarrelled. I couldn't argue about his dad though, that guy gave me the creeps too.

"The guy is whiter than a ghost and has no friends; I'd say that's a little weird," Johnny stuck to his guns.

"Freak is a strong word," I tried to make some sort of argument, but I couldn't deny he was a bit odd.

"I think he's mysterious," Jade sighed with a lustful smile.

"He's a loner," Stephanie snorted.

"You still fancy him though, don't ya?" Sofia barked.

"So do you!" She hissed in retaliation.

"Easy tigers!" Johnny intervened, trying to hide the look of disappointment and jealousy on his face. "This van is a no-drama-zone!"

"Why don't we listen to some music to pass the time?" Dotty suggested after a few minutes of an awkward silence.

"Good idea!" Johnny sighed with relief as he hastily switched on the radio. His face looked sad. Probably the realization that he's not the only man in Stephanie's lovely blue eyes, although I imagine she made him feel as though he were the only one, stroking his ego among other things. I imagine she can be quite convincing when in full flirt-mode.

I thanked my lucky stars that I had gotten in the minivan after Dotty, who now sat squashed awkwardly between Sofia and Jade, and because of that I had a window seat.

I lusted at the dense green forests that edged the road outside the castle. Then we drove through the grey lifeless town. I grimaced at the flashback of those things with red eyes that me and Linx had hidden from when I fist arrived, which seemed like an eternity ago now.

Soon we were past the dreary town and the road curled off into greenery again. Grassy-dense-forest stalked the path that sneaked around a gorgeous blue river that eventually gushed into a huge breathtaking lake. The swirling water was a dark blue-almost-grey. The reflection of the sun sparkled across it as though someone had dipped orange and yellow Inc into it. I looked in aw as the dark-grey water white-caped gracefully in and out of the rocks. It splashed swiftly and gently against the orange tinted cliffs. It was a picture postcard moment as the lake swept across the sandy shores, creating white foam as it heaved softly back and fourth. Islands rose in uneven summits from the steel waters, with sheer cliff sides that were crowned with soaring austere firs. Large smooth stones carpeted most of the beach, leaving just a thin layer of greyish-yellow sand that lined between the stones and the water. It looked incredible as each stone had a different shade of colour. Sea-green, dull-gold, lavender, terracotta, blue-grey, they sparkled under the sunlight like crystals. Strewn across the tide line were huge driftwood trees that had been bleached a sort of bone-white by the sun and salt waves. Some were stacked together, piling up against the edge of the woodland fringe, adding to the mystical image of the forest, and the others were lying in solitary, just out of reach of the whooshing foamy salt waves that licked the shores. A cool and briny brisk breeze came off of the waves, flickering gorgeously against our faces. Floating on the swells were Pelicans. Seagulls swiftly glided above them. In the distance soaring high beyond the clouds that circled the sky, threatening to invade at any moment and ruin our sunshine, lurked a lone eagle, wheeling effortlessly though the atmosphere. I was grateful that the sun continued to shine bravely, pinning back the dense clouds with its halo of blue sky, but couldn't help thinking it was only a matter of time before the clouds outnumbered the fierce ball of raging fire, suffocating it's flame whose warmth brushed my appreciative body benevolently.

Being careful not to tumble over the driftwood logs that had obviously been used for parties, we made our way across the beach with Stephanie leading the charge. There was a fire circle filled with black ashes and a few empty beer cans. Stacy and a few of her female cronies were there, perched on one of the bone-coloured benches. They were glowering at us as we approached. Some boys appeared and Johnny abandoned us to join them. The girls all clustered together in different packs, gossiping, whispering and giggling excitedly. Whilst the men begun to gather broken branches of driftwood from the drier piles in and around the woods. They soon had some sort of tepee-shaped construction built atop of the old cinders and had begun to light it up with a cigarette lighter. The fire rapidly licked up and around all the dry wood, blazing it into a beautiful stunning blue flame.

"Why is it blue?" I gasped with astonishment.

"It's the salt," Johnny explained as he came and sat between me and Stephanie. She glared at me territorial-like as she turned to him and claimed his attention. I rolled my eyes and turned to talk to Sofia, Jade, Estella and Dotty.

Stacy shook out her golden locks and eyed me scornfully.

"It's so pretty," Dotty sighed as she watched the strange green and blue fire crackle toward the sky.

"Here we go," Sofia chuckled to herself with an eye roll as she watched the boys strip off down to their underwear.

"That didn't take long," Estella scoffed.

"Who's up for a hike to the tidal pools?" A boy yelled eagerly. Johnny leapt up like an excited puppy and I couldn't help but snigger at Stacy who wasn't wearing the right shoes for a hike. I wasn't going to go, but then when I realised Stacy wasn't going, that made my decision for me. Dotty, Stephanie and Estella stayed back at the beach with most of the other girls, whilst I, Sofia and Jade, followed the group of boys through the forest.

"I'm surprised Stephanie didn't come, especially when Johnny is coming," Jade said, "She clearly likes him."

"No Jade!" Sofia groaned, "He serves a purpose. He has a minivan."

"Oh she's not *that* shallow, surely?" Jade replied.

"I think she might be," I sided with Sofia.

"That's not nice," Jade grumbled.

"I am surprised she didn't come though, if I am honest, as she did seem a bit jealous when Johnny spoke to me by the fire. She quickly claimed him," I moaned.

"Oh, that's just Stephanie marking her territory; staking claim to what she assumes is hers. I'd flirt with him just to wind her up," Sofia sniggered.

"No way, if I do that she'll do the same with Linx and Lingwood," I frowned as I said both their names like they were mine.

"She'll do that anyway," Sofia sighed, "She just can't help herself."

"I thought you said you liked Stephanie?" Jade challenged Sofia.

"Her hearts in the right place, but I wouldn't trust her around someone I liked," Sofia asserted.

"I can't imagine you liking anyone!" Jade bitched.

Sofia frowned and continued walking.

"You're brave," I gasped to Jade.

"Sorry," Jade apologised, probably realising that she was lucky not to get her nose broken, "I didn't mean to be nasty."

Sofia shrugged and continued her usual frown.

"KEEP UP!" The boys yelled as they hiked on ahead of us like a wolf-pack of topless Tarzans. We giggled to ourselves as we listened to their random shouts and grunts of excitement, along with their banter and laughter.

"Boys are so competitive," Jade sighed as she shook her head.

"Small things amuse small minds," Sofia giggled.

We all laughed and picked up the pace to try and catch up with the lads.

After stumbling over various roots that hooked the floor, rocks that erected sharply from nowhere, mud-hills that randomly plummeted, and ducking low branches, we finally broke through the emerald foliage of the confined forest, emerging back out to the rocky shore again. We hadn't travelled far, but I was relieved to see the blue sky once more. The green lights of the forest and the shadows caused by the trees that roofed above us, made it chilly and dark. I was grateful to feel the warm touch of the sun rays back on my chalky-skin.

It was a low tide, and a stripe little tidal river trickled past us on its way to the sea. Shallow pools that weren't completely drained along the pebbled banks were swarming with life. I was spellbound by the natural aquarium that swirled bellow me in the small ocean ponds. Brilliant anemones, like rows of bouquets, rippled eternally in the invisible current. I was completely absorbed as I took in the images. Starfish scattered the black rocks motionless like stars against the night sky. Twisted shells with crabs inside them scurried around the edges. And I wowed at a thin black eel waiting for the sea to return as it waved its way through the rocks and bright green weeds.

Jade and I slowly and carefully hid amongst the trees as we stripped off to our swimwear. We were both very cautious not to lean over too far or step too eagerly, whereas Sofia had ripped off her clothes and was already in her bathing-suit. She fearlessly dived right in with the boys. They leapt over the slippery rocks, splashing into the pools.

"Are you two coming in?" Sofia yelled.

Suddenly from nowhere a cheeky boy placed his palm onto her head, dunking her under the water. Jade and I looked at each other with open-mouthed-expressions as Sofia bobbled back up gasping for air and choking on the salty water. The fiery bald-headed-girl instantly re-submerged, tugging the boys shorts down with such force that she almost ripped them off. He splashed and squirmed as he tried to pull them back up, but everyone saw what was on the menu.

"Cute!" The boy growled, unimpressed as he yanked them back up.

"Not as cute as *that* little thing," Sofia giggled, glancing down towards his crotch. The boy went bright red as everybody laughed and then Sofia cut him some slack, when she finally left him alone to come over to us.

"Can't believe you just did that," Jade gasped.

Sofia shrugged.

"Oh my god, he's coming over!" I wheezed.

"What?" Sofia whispered as a shot of panic spread over her face.

"I'm Tom," he introduced himself to Sofia.

"And I'm not interested," she replied bluntly.

"That's an odd name," he sniggered.

She ignored him.

"I just wanted to apologise for the dunk," he said.

"Why? It's just banter," Sofia smiled, "Besides, I got my own back."

"You certainly did," he laughed as he came alongside her, "So do you have anyone to take you to the dance?"

Sofia burst out laughing.

"What?" She asked bewilderedly after she had composed herself. Me and Jade both giggled too, not meaning it horribly, just out of shock.

"If you haven't been asked then I'd like to take you to the dance," he said confidently.

"Dunking a girl under water and then asking her to a dance, that's a new one," Jade whispered to me.

"No offence, but I've seen all I need to see, and I am *not* interested," she snickered heartlessly as she wiggled her little finger.

Mine and Jade's jaws both hit the ground.

To be fair to the guy he handled her well, hiding his embarrassment and blush almost to the point where I questioned if it had even existed.

"I'm a grower not a shower," he winked at her, "If you change your mind then come and find me. Have a nice day," he then swam off.

"That was brutal Sofia!" Jade snapped. "You could have let him down a bit nicer."

Sofia nodded and for once didn't retaliate. I was really impressed at how well he handled that. Most guys would have responded badly to the rejection, especially in such a mocking fashion, but Tom was as cool as a cucumber. Even more surprisingly was that Sofia looked as though she wanted to burst into tears.

"Are you ok?" I asked her.

She nodded and her eyes begun to water slightly. Now me and Jade had both climbed into the pool to hug her.

"I'm fine!" She said as she tried to push us off.

"No you're not," we both insisted as we forced the hug on her.

"I said I'm fine!" She snarled angrily, but her voice lacked its usual intimidation as an uncontrollable sob made it squeak. We both hugged her tight.

"He's not looking, is he?" She fretted as she tried to hold back her cry.

"No," Jade reassured her.

"I think I'll go and apologise to him," she said as she dried her eyes, "I *was* a bit harsh."

My heart warmed to see this side of Sofia. She wasn't as tough as she made out and it made me just want to hug her even tighter. Although, I also think Sofia was very impressed at how well he had handled her rejection.

"He's with his friends, I'll apologise later," she promised.

"I've never seen you this vulnerable, what's going on?" Jade asked with concern.

"I'm bald," she blurted angrily, "It makes me ugly . . . Inside, and out!"

"Well, *he* obviously doesn't think that Sofia," Jade reassured her, "And you're not ugly."

"You're beautiful!" I added.

"How do you know it's not a dare?" She growled, but her usual temper lacked conviction as her bottom lip trembled slightly.

"Since when do *you* care what people think?" I blurted.

"I don't!" She insisted as she composed herself and climbed out, "I'm heading back to the beach now, you coming?"

We both nodded and got out.

"Leaving so soon girls?" Some boys called out to us.

"Yeah, we're hungry," Jade lied.

"What you hungry for? Perhaps we can help?" One of the boys sniggered with his mates as he grabbed his crotch.

"Sorry small-muscles, we ain't interested!" Sofia seemed back to her usual brutal self.

"We weren't talking to you baldy!" He retaliated.

"Sorry, I didn't understand that, I don't speak idiot," Sofia chuckled, but I could see the bald comment hurt her, even if she hid it well.

"If I wanted a bitch I'd get a dog," he laughed, "Probably would be better looking too."

"Hey, dick!" Tom intervened, "Don't speak to her like that!"

Me and Jade caught a glimpse of Sofia's smirk before she quickly hid it.

"Stay out of this Tom!" The boy warned.

"Talk to her like that again and I'll punch you square on the nose. Got it?" Tom threatened.

"Yeah?!" The guy yelled, "Bring it!!!"

"Don't punch his nose. If the rumours are true then he's only just fixed it," Sofia called out.

"What?" The boy laughed mockingly.

"You ran into a wall with an erection and broke your nose, didn't you?" Sofia said with a straight face, "Coz that's the rumour. So don't punch him on that delicate small nose of his . . . Come on girls, let's leave Tiny-Tim with his small *everything*, and go get us some food," she said as she strutted on ahead, leaving everyone laughing at the boy.

"This isn't over Tom!" I heard the boy threaten as we followed Sofia through the forest.

"I love you Sofia!" I giggled, "That was awesome."

"I spotted that smile when Tom defended you," Jade sniggered.

"I don't know what you're talking about," Sofia grumbled.

"Do you like him?" We asked.

"No!" She blushed.

"Oh my god, you totally do!" We both squealed excitedly and Sofia didn't reply.

"What's wrong?" Jade asked.

"You said so yourself Jade! You couldn't imagine me liking anyone. Well it's true, and I don't like you either! So back off before I make you back off. Final warning!" Sofia threatened.

"Are you ok?" I asked, ignoring her threat to Jade. Jade however looked a little upset.

Sofia suddenly stopped dead in her tracks and turned sharply to me and Jade. She seemed a little hostile, making Jade flinch. "Look! I know I am bald and angry, but I'm still female, I still need a cry once in a while! Now get over it, coz I am!" And then she stomped off.

Me and Jade didn't buy that she *was* ok, but we knew the best thing we could do for Sofia was to give her-her space, so we leisurely strolled behind her, leaving Sofia with her frustrations.

When we returned to the beach, the small crowd we had left behind had multiplied. As I got closer I noticed that I hadn't seen them before. The teenage newcomers had shiny blonde hair and copper skin. I went and sat with Estella in the driftwood circle, whilst food got passed around between everybody. The choice was different sandwiches and an array of sodas to pick from. The sandy soggy sandwiches reminded me of a time many years ago when my mum and I were on a beach. I was only little, but it was a fond memory of better times. I suddenly felt a ray of sadness sweep over me as I thought about how much I missed my mum.

"Hi, I'm Harry," one of the new boys said as he plonked himself down beside me, reaching his hand out in a friendly gesture. He looked fifteen, maybe sixteen years old, and had long glossy blonde hair tied back tightly with string at the nape of his neck. His skin was golden and beautifully tanned, silky and milk-coffee-coloured. His eyes were dark brown, set high above his cheekbones, and his teeth glistened whiter than a Hollywood-Stars-grin against the backdrop of his copper skin. He had a very handsome face.

"I'm Eleni," I placed my palm inside his warm grip.

He shook gently and then released our hands. The slight stick of his warm flesh clung to mine as we disengaged and I had a strange feeling of not wanting it to end.

"It's nice to meet you Eleni," he said with a beaming grin that was so white it almost made me squint, "You wouldn't remember me, but you used to hang out with my sisters, I think you were friends," he claimed.

I frowned in deep thought.

"Chloe and Danz?" He chuckled.

"Oh, wow, yeah," I suddenly recalled.

My dad hardly had time for me on the months that I was forced to come here by the courts, and he had thrown me with a few babysitters, and that's where I met Chloe and Danz. They were only a year or two older than me, and we briefly played together to pass the time. I wouldn't tell Harry this, but we were hardly friends.

"Are they here?" I examined the girls around the beach. "How are they?"

His face dropped to a puppy-dog expression.

"Chloe died in a car crash a few years back, and Danz moved away. I think she lives in Florida now with her boyfriend."

"Oh, I'm so sorry," I comforted.

"It's ok," he shrugged.

"How are your parents . . . Clive, and, err . . . Monty?" I asked.

He looked really awkward, "Clive and Monty were not my parents."

"Oh, I always assumed . . . I'm sorry," I sighed with sadness.

"Yeah . . . err," he paused. "My parents died in an animal attack when I was too young to remember them . . . and . . . err . . . about that car crash with Chloe. Both my uncles were in that car too. Monty was the only survivor, but he's not like you'd remember," he pointed out sadly.

My heart sank and I could have cried for him there and then.

"I'm so sorry to hear that Harry, I really am. How is Monty different?"

"He's in a wheelchair," he described with a shrug, "I look after him."

"On your own?" I gasped with concern.

"My brother Linx swings by most days. He helps bath him and drops off food, but it's mainly me looking after him," Harry explained.

"Oh, your brother is Linx?" I blushed.

"Yeah. I hope one day I can be just like him," Harry admitted. "So, do you know him?"

"He's one of my teachers up at the castle," I said awkwardly.

"Oh that's cool. So do you like his car?" Harry grinned.

"I love it," I smiled.

"I was so relieved when Linx took it, so I could start building another car," he sighed.

"You build cars?" I asked, impressed.

"When I have the occasional spare time after school or weekends, and the right parts, then yes, I build cars," he grinned proudly.

"That's really cool," I complimented.

"You wouldn't happen to know where I could get my hands on an Aventador LP700-4 2012 non start-stop system, by any chance?" He added jokingly. He had a very pleasant and husky voice.

"Sorry," I laughed, "I haven't seen any lately, but I'll keep my eyes open for you," I joked. As if I even knew what that thing was. Just like his brother, Harry was very easy to talk to.

"Linx's car is really slow though," he smirked.

"It's not slow!" I objected, as I remembered when he picked me up from the airport, we reached some pretty nifty speeds.

"It is compared to my Lamborghini that I'm working on," he grinned.

My chin almost hit the sand, "You're building a Lamborghini?"

"Well, not from scratch. I'm fixing it up for a friend. He has two of them and says if I fix them both, then I can keep one," he blurted excitedly, "Once I learn to drive and get my licence that is."

"That's so cool!" I expressed.

He flashed his brilliant smile and glared appreciatively at me for slightly longer than I felt comfortable, but then I was beginning to get used to these strange looks that boys kept giving me. Especially since my hairs grown slightly longer lately, I've noticed a few glances; it was down past my ears now. I decided I wanted to grow it since I met Stephanie and was jealous of her long thick red mane that curled down to her butt. I knew I wouldn't get it that long though, as my hair tends to split at its ends when I let it grow too far, but nonetheless, I decided to give it a go. Another valid reason for me not to cut it back to its usual boyish look, also, was the coldness here. Back in Blosoms Hill the sun was so hot that it seemed silly for me to have longer hair. But not here! If anything it would be nice to have long feminine hair to scarf my neck and keep me warm.

"What's your secret," I whispered, "How do you get your hair so long and lovely-looking?"

Harry blushed red in the face, "Lots of salty seawater and plenty of sunshine," he recommended.

"Sunshine, round these parts?" I snorted.

"The clouds only cover the castle and town," he pointed out. "Where I live we have plenty."

"Oh, and where do you live?" I asked.

"Just over that cliff," he pointed to some sort of mountain that erected from the lake.

"That's not far," I complained, "How comes there is sun there and not here?"

He turned to see if anyone was listening or watching and then leaned in close to me and whispered, "The Devil's gate draws the doomsday clouds over the town and castle. It makes it cold and rainy, but outside the perimeter, it is lovely and warm."

"You know about the devils gate?" My eyes glared with surprise.

"Shhhhhhh!" He hushed me, "Not many outsiders know it exists."

"Well how do you know?" I whispered back.

"I overheard my brother talking about it once and confronted him. He made me promise not to tell anyone, but I knew you'd know, so it's ok," he smiled.

"How did you know that I'd know?"

"You're from the castle," he grinned, Stadley Hold, or I suppose these days it's Stadley Hall."

"Why did they change the name?" I asked.

"They didn't really. Some people call it Stadley Hold, and some call it Stadley Hall. I guess it's both names," he shrugged.

Harry was the most smiley person I had ever met, and you couldn't help but get roped in and grin back. I was beginning to think nothing could wipe the grin off of his face - when suddenly an insolent voice did just that.

"You missing Lingwood yet Eleni," Stacy smeared my name.

"Is that your boyfriend?" Harry asked with an alerted and slight jealous tone.

"No," I replied.

"But she'd like him to be," Stacy giggled, "Or is it Linx?"

"My brother?" Harry gasped.

"Look, I'm single!" I snapped and then regretted it, as it sounded like I wanted Harry to know.

He tried to hide his delight.

"How do you two know each other?" Stacy asked.

"I've known Eleni since I was born," he laughed, smiling at me again.

"How nice," she said, trying to sound sincere, in the most unconvincing sincere tone I had ever heard. She didn't sound like she thought it was nice at all.

"The Putin's don't come here!" Another boy grumbled in a tone that made it sound like they weren't allowed.

"Why?" I asked and Harry hushed me again.

Stacy was soon pulled away by another group of boys who all fought for her attention.

"That must be exhausting having to fight off all those boys constantly," I joked.

"She seems to like it," Harry chuckled a response, causing me to laugh.

"Why did you hush me just now?" I asked.

"Walk with me," he insisted as he got up, lending his warm grip to me once again, to help me up. I placed my palm into his toasty-clutch once more and he tugged me up.

"Your hands are so soft," he complimented as he held on a little longer than he needed to, allowing his fingers to brush mine as I slipped out.

"Thanks," I said a little awkwardly.

"Come on," he said as he walked on ahead.

"Where are we going?" I asked as I glanced back towards Sofia and the other girls who all watched me like a hawk.

"Away from the eavesdropping," he explained.

I raised an eyebrow and curiously followed him down the beach. As we strolled across the multitude of beautiful stones and sand, heading toward the driftwood seawall at the foot of the forest, the clouds swooped in, finally shutting up shop and blocking the sun. The sea immediately darkened and the temperature plummeted.

"So, is Stadley Hall driving you crazy yet?" He made small talk.

"Understatement," I grimaced as I hugged my arms for warmth.

He grinned understandingly but still didn't get to the point as of why we were walking down the beach, to my frustration, as I shivered slightly.

"Here, take my jacket," he insisted, and before I could refuse he had flung it around my shoulders.

"Thanks," I mumbled.

"How old are you?" He asked me.

"How old do you think I am?" I smirked, enjoying watching the panic flare across his face.

"Errr," he gulped.

"That's why you should never ask a girl how old they are," I chuckled, "You get yourself into trouble."

"Noted," he grinned, a little embarrassed.

"And it is rude!" I said sharply, but I was teasing.

He nodded with a smirk, unfazed by my attempt at making him squirm some more.

"So . . . ?"

"So what?" I frowned.

"Your age," he grinned.

"I'm seventeen," I sighed with an eye roll, "You?"

"I just turned fifteen," he confessed.

"You look older," I said with surprise.

"I'm tall and have muscle, that's why," he said cockily as he tensed his bicep. It wasn't as big or as firm as his older brothers, but I could still appreciate it nonetheless.

"Cocky much?" I joked.

"Very," he winked at me.

"You're very assured of yourself for such a young pup," I said, trying not to blush at his piercing eyes that were undressing me.

"And you're very pretty," he complimented.

"I'm too old for you," I bluntly put an end to it, "Why did we walk out here?"

He handled the rejection well, hiding the disappointment in his eyes, which was an attractive quality.

"Can't blame a guy for trying," he made light of it, a personality trait of his that I was beginning to grow really fond of.

I smiled, "You're cute. You'll have them queuing up for you," I promised.

"You think I'm cute? There is hope for me yet," he chuckled cheekily.

I rolled my eyes.

"Just get to the point of why we are out here, as the weather is turning and I'll probably have to leave soon," I said eagerly.

Finally he got to the point, "You promise not to tell anyone?"

"I promise," I replied.

He smiled, looking allured as he gazed deep into my eyes. I was flattered by this young crush he had on me, but I didn't want to lead him on, nor be too harsh. I wanted to look away but his stare held my attention for a little longer than I should had let it, as his dark brown eyes glistened almost gold and were smouldering at me. I quickly blushed and looked away as I let out a sigh.

"Do you like scary tales?" His husky voice asked portentously.

I nodded slowly, still feeling a little shocked at how much I enjoyed being around him.

His broad lips smiled as we sat down on some nearby driftwood.

"Do you know the tale of the Putin's and The Greenwoods?" He begun.

"No," I admitted as I shook my head.

"Well, there are many myths and old-wives-tales out there – but, according to legend round these parts, there was a feud between two families – The Greenwood's and The Putin's. They hated each other and it was a grudge that dated back centuries. They fought over land and anything they could, and they didn't care who got caught in the crossfire. Now, according to legend, they spilled so much innocent blood in their disputes with each other, that a powerful witch cursed them, turning them into creatures of the night. The Greenwoods controlled by the moon and the Putin's controlled by the sun, they were known as Hair-beasts and Blood-drinkers," he paused to look at me before continuing, "Or as modern myths have come to know them as . . . Werewolves and Vampires."

"Oh stop!" I groaned, "You expect me to believe that?"

"Well, it is just a story, but that is the reason Lingwood and his father will never step foot on this beach. The Putin's hunted down The Greenwoods at night in their vampire form and killed them all, except a few that escaped. Then the next full moon came and the last remaining Greenwoods hunted the Vampires down in Werewolf form, getting their revenge and slaughtering them, until only a few remained. My great-grandfather, Harrison Greenwood, who I am named after, made a truce with Vladiminr Putin and his son Lingwood. If they would stay at Stadley Hold and stop tormenting the world with their terror and hunger to feed on humans, then the wolves would leave them alone and not expose them to the world," he winked at me. "That's the legend."

"The animal attacks," I mumbled under my breath.

"The what?" He asked.

"Look, I got to go now. Thank you for a wonderful story," I said kindly.

He smirked a crooked grin, "You think I'm nuts now don't ya?"

"A little," I said playfully.

"My family believe it. Linx believes it," he asserted passionately.

"Given everything I have seen up at the castle and beyond the gates, I don't *not* believe it," I reassured him, "I just have to go now, the rain is coming!"

"Ok," he sighed.

"I had a really great time with you," I blurted without thinking and regretted the compliment, fearing I was giving him the wrong impression.

His grin stretched across his face, "Me too," he beamed cheerfully, "I'll walk you back."

"Ok," I shrugged as I put the hood up on his jacket that he had leant me, as the rain began to spit.

"When I get my licence, would you like to come for a ride with me?" He asked.

"Sure I would, especially in a Lamborghini," I laughed.

"I bet Linx would be jealous!" He sniggered.

I hope so – I found myself smirking at the thought. Then I frowned and banished the dreadful thought, I wouldn't want to make anybody jealous, that's just cruel.

"Why would he be jealous?" I asked.

"A pretty girl, a nicer car than his, what's not to be jealous of?" He grinned cheekily.

I smiled back contently, "Harry, I'm sure you'll have plenty of pretty girls your own age by the time you come to get your licence."

"Maybe I like more mature girls," he flirted.

I blushed and couldn't help a grin, "You're like a dog on heat," I chuckled.

"Well, my ancestors *are* wolves, supposedly," he winked at me.

"Well, down boy!" I joked.

"I can roll over for you and let you rub my belly if you like? And other things," he flirted.

"I won't be rubbing anything," I asserted sternly, "Nice try though."

I had to give him ten out of ten for effort and I was a little flattered.

When we got back to the group, everyone was packing away. I noticed Tom and a group of lads were heading towards us.

"See you around Eleni," Harry caught me off guard as he leant in and planted one right on my cheek as he hugged me. His lips felt soft, warm, and gentle. I got a waft of whatever aftershave he was wearing, and it smelt so good I considered gripping him in a bear hug just so I could sniff his neck, as he broke away from me.

"Bye," I said, handing him his jacket back.

He grinned and jogged up the beach and out of sight. He was an attractive boy, but far too young for me, yet I found myself admiring him as he jogged away.

"Hey," a man's voice called out to me, breaking my glare.

I turned round to see a tall, slim and fairly-good-looking man with high cheekbones, a sharp nose and seductive green eyes. His short brown hair swirled and curled in the wind.

"Hi Tom," I smiled, "Are you looking for Sofia?"

"Yeah, I am. I've not seen her since I got back from the shallow pools," he replied.

I glanced around, "I don't see her either," I frowned.

"We've not been properly introduced, you know my name but I don't know yours?" He held out his hand.

"I'm Eleni," I gently shook his hand.

"Nice to meet you Eleni. Could you give this to Sofia please," he handed me a bit of paper with his phone number on it.

"Sure I can," I smiled.

"Thanks," he nodded and walked away.

Suddenly from nowhere that rude boy from the shallow pools marched towards him, he had a gang of five mates with him.

"I told you this wasn't over, Tom!" He yelled.

"Is this how you settle your disputes, Darren, six against one?" Tom grumbled.

"If you offend one of us, then you offend all of us," the man I now know to be Darren, said as he foamed at the mouth.

A crowd built up instantly to observe the potential fight. I noticed Sofia coming back from the minivan with Dotty and Stephanie in the distance.

Suddenly a punch was thrown by one of Darren's cronies. Tom blocked it impressively and countered with a great hook, sending the teenager plunging towards the sand – but, Tom was outnumbered, and despite getting a few nice blocks and counter punches in, the gang soon got the better of him. A cracking sound as Darren's knuckles connected with Tom's jaw made my heart skip.

Dramatically Sofia appeared, running in with a rock held firmly in her small hand. The 5ft-nothing girl jumped far above the ground as she reached high to smash it into the side of one of the boy's heads, clearing a path to Darren. She leapt impressively and somehow mounted the 6ft frame of Darren, clinging to his back and ripping at his hair.

"Get off me!" He snarled as he threw her to the floor with ease. He picked up a thick branch of driftwood that was lying on the beach. "I'm going to hurt you now, shiny head!" He threatened.

"Well, you'll have to go through me!" Dotty shouted as she ran to stand next to Sofia who was climbing to her feet.

Darren laughed.

"And me!" Estella suddenly stood next to Sofia and Dotty.

Feeling energised by my friends and furious at this boy and his gang of thugs, I took my queue to also run and stand next to them.

"And me!" I tried to make my voice as deep and as angry as I could.

Jade then leapt in with her fists raised, "And me!"

To our surprise Stephanie strutted in and took up a stance next to us. "Sorry boys, I'm not just a pretty face. This kitty-cat has claws!" She hissed.

I couldn't help but smile as Darren took a step back, dragging his pal who had been struck with the rock, back to his feet. The boy looked a little dazed but seemed ok.

"Hell yeah to girl power!" Tom chanted as he also climbed to his feet.

Darren turned to face the chant, turning straight into it. Everybody heard the snapping crunch of his nose as it broke like a twig from the impact of Tom's waiting fist.

I almost screeched in excitement when the punch connected as the adrenalin flooded through my veins.

"Aghhhhhhhhhhh," Darren cried as he held his bleeding nose.

"Oh no, not the nose," Sofia laughed as Darren's mates escorted him away.

Tom turned to her in a panting voice, "I like you and I want to take you to the dance!"

Caught off guard by his fearless and directness, Sofia blushed a smile, something that was rarer than rocking-horse-droppings. "Not interested," she said as she snatched the bit of paper off of me that had his number on it and strutted past him. I could have sworn she was exaggerating the wiggle of her hips for his benefit as she walked up the beach towards the minivan.

Tom turned to look at me with an unsure expression. Sofia must had seen him give me the bit of paper, which means she was watching him, and she took the paper, so she clearly doesn't want to dispose of his phone number. This made me smile. She was so obviously playing hard to get. I gave Tom an encouraging thumbs-up with a nod.

"I think you might be getting a text later," I giggled.

The group of us then left him on the beach to go catch up with Sofia. Johnny had already started up the engine by the time we arrived at the van and on the journey back to the castle I couldn't help but think and wonder if there is any truth to those *scary tales* . . .

5- BROKEN TRUCE

Linx found himself thinking back to the days when Stone Chasers were taken for granted – The days where Stone Chasers were many and not considered an endangered species - The days when enchanting stones were far easier to find – The days when things were far simpler.

He was just a young lad when he started out, and like most young lads, he selfishly loathed in his own suffering, not caring for the bigger picture, just the laziness of the here and now. He was lost in the misery of his work, barely even aware of his surroundings. Long despairing sighs escaped him every time the Swords had glowed brightly to let them know that stones were somewhere in the vicinity. Sores and blisters caked his tender feet. His young-and-still-growing-muscles protested throughout his legs from the hikes through the rough terrain of the caves, the glow of the swords leading the way, getting brighter the nearer they got. Once they found the location where the swords had guided them to, a new pain would be added on top of his already distraught limbs. His underdeveloped juvenile muscles in his arms now ached alongside his legs, from the endless pounding of the Hydraulic Jackhammer. Small splints of stone and rock flicked up off of the cavern walls as he burrowed through with the drill, the tiny boulders and granite ricocheting off of his protective-goggles, stinging his exposed face and hands. Atomized dust flooded his lungs as it filled the air, obscuring his vision. His ears felt as though they were bleeding from all the grime and rock particles settling in his canal, not to mention the ringing and screeching whine of the jack. The horrible hum filled the cavern which was slowly beginning to burst his eardrums. The agonising drone of the drilling noise drowned out any other sounds as it grinded and twisted deeper and deeper, burrowing centimetre by agonizing centimetre into the thick core of the limestone.

Linx could see the magical veins of the mythical stones that were woven deep inside the centre of the crumbling and cracking rocks and he bored through them. They had been called many different names throughout the centuries – Magic Stones, Mythical Stones, Lazarus Stones – But Linx knew them as Power Stones. Impervious to both heat and energy meant the stones were indestructible. They had to remain a secret from the world. If Earth discovered their existence, then the stones would become a prize in the construction of armour and various weapons by both commercial and military contractors, and god knows what else. Each individual stone had the potential, if in the wrong hands, to weald the power of one-hundred nuclear bombs. So they remain a heavily guarded kept secret. Fortunately the special stones could only be discovered near the gates of hell, which was protected by Stadley Hold, so they weren't likely to be stumbled upon by an outsider. On the downside though, being next to Hell made it a very dangerous and a hostile place to mine. Demons more than often attacked which was why Holy-Men stood on the outskirts of the mines to protect the Stone-Chasers. – A luxury that they no longer have these days.

Unfortunately, the very properties that made these stones so valuable also made the stones extremely difficult to mine. Any form of flame deemed useless and the magical stones propelled almost everything. In the old days before electronics, it would take days, even weeks to scrape off just the smallest of magic-laced rock. Fortunately nowadays electronic breakers existed, as the only real affective way to get big chunks off was through the brute force of the hydraulic jack pounding relentlessly away, chipping it free bit by bit. The problem was that the force of the pounding would quickly wear down a head of a jack, blunting it until it became almost useless. The dirt and dust would clog the hydraulic pistons, making them jam. Mining for Magical-Power-Stones was hard on equipment, but as Linx soon discovered was even harder on the workmen. And then there were the demon attacks. Holy-men did what they could to protect the miners, but every so often you'd hear a scream from one of the caves and then just find the remains of a Stone Chaser, or sometimes nothing at all. It was a scary place to be. The tunnels claimed many, burying bodies in *cave-ins or incinerating them when somebody drilled into a pocket of steaming volatile gases ensnared in the rock. There has even been times when the grounds given way, sending miners tumbling into a bottomless black tomb. And even those that did survive and made it out to a grand older age, there was no retirement and they often found that decades of hard physical labour and exposure to airborne contaminants took its toll. Any young man that worked the mines got big. The mines would transform a younger man into a mountain of muscle with heavy hands and broad shoulders. But as you got older the mass of hard knotted bodies eventually crippled. Older men would suddenly drop dead in the caves from exhaustion as sixty-year-old men were left with broken shells worn down over time, bodies that looked and felt like they were ninety, often dying of heart failure.*

Few Stone Chasers ever reached their golden years. But Linx had all that to look forward to.

The young lad had been hammering away for nearly eight standard hours. The huge drill weighed more than forty kilos, and the awful strain it took to keep it pressed and raised against the rock-face was wrecking his mind and body to the point of utter shut down.

His exhausted arms and hands trembled from the exertion. His head pounded as though it was getting hit with a sledge-hammer every couple of seconds. His back protested from the constant bending beginning to take its toll. His lungs were begging for clean oxygen as they gasped desperately for air, choking on the constant clouds of fine mineral dust thrown up from the head of the drill. The rattling vibration even hurt his teeth as the constant shuddering from the jack almost shook them loose from his gums.

But the Witches and Wizards paid them well, and kept their family members safe from the illnesses and diseases of the world, allowing them to have a natural fulfilled healthy life. If a Stone Chaser refused his or her duty, then they'd be imprisoned and their family left to starve and to rely on non-magical healthcare. Their payment, despite the minimal payment being generous, also varied based on how much stone they brought back, meaning that there wasn't a limit on the maximum payment a Stone Chaser could receive. Linx knew very well that he could potentially be a very wealthy man. The problem was, a Stone Chaser wasn't a job you could just retire from, it was a job for life. No good having money if you spend your days and nights in a cave drilling forever. The whine of the hydraulic motor took on a higher pitch and Linx rolled his eyes as he recognised the moaning sound all too well. After roughly twenty-thousand rotations per minute and the weight of him constantly pushing through the toughest rock unknown to man, the motor begun to malfunction, as he knew it would. It began sucking in dust like a thirsty Camel lapping up water after fifteen days of a long desert crossing. The only way to combat this problem was by regular cleaning and servicing, something the headmaster didn't like them to do. He'd rather chuck it away and buy cheap equipment than risk drawing attention to the mining activities that go on at Stadley Hold by sinking credits into regular maintenance. Of course he could magically compel people to forget, but it is the stones that create the magic and therefore would be a misuse and waste of their precious power. So the headmaster would rather rely on the old fashioned – lying, avoid and deception – techniques, rather than magic. Linx of course, however, would rather buy an expensive drill and chuck a few quid at it every-now-and-then to get the damn thing serviced. Rather than keep buying cheap replacements, but those sorts of decisions were way above his pay grade. The headmaster thought different, and that was that.

Despite being young and relatively inexperienced, Linx had been around the jackhammers long enough to recognise their despairing cry for help, and he knew what was going to happen next – and a second later, it did. The pleading machine died as the motor finally blew. The hydraulics growled and grizzled its last whining plea as it seized with a horrible crunch, and then a cloud of black smoke spat from the rear. Linx released his cramped finger from the trigger and threw the digger to the floor, the scorching bit of useless equipment clonked loudly echoing through the caves as it collided with the uneven rocky ground.

Linx turned around as a shadow dimmed the light for a second. He suddenly realised nobody else was in the cave but him, no other Stone Chasers.

"Hello! Who's there?" He called out.

"A Greenwood all alone near the gates of hell," a frosty whisper chillingly spoke from the shadows.

"Show yourself!" Linx demanded.

A tall slim man stepped into the light, his long dark hair, dark eyebrows and dark goatee beard stood prominent against the backdrop of his white-chalk-skin.

"Vladimir Putin!" Linx gasped.

The man smiled a blood red grin, revealing his sharp fangs.

"You know a bite from a Werewolf is the only thing that can split the skin of a Vampire and kill you," Linx reminded.

"Yes," he laughed, "And I don't see one here," he looked around mockingly, "And you know that your kind are powerless against the vampire when it isn't a full moon," his grin widened as he took a step closer.

"If you want to break the truce and attack me, then you know you'll suffer the consequences on the next full moon," Linx warned.

"I and your grandfather made that truce, and he is long gone now. You think I fear you and your young brother?" He sniggered, "Two little puppies," his smile widened even more as he said it.

"What about my mum and dad and my two uncles," Linx said confidently.

"You have one uncle," Vladimir corrected, "The other man is his lover. Besides, haven't you heard the news Linx?" His eyes widened with delight.

"Whatever . . . What news?" Linx frowned.

"Haven't you wondered where all your Stone Chaser friends have vanished to?" He took another step closer, "Leaving you all alone in a big dangerous cave next to the gates of Satan, it's a bit irresponsible, wouldn't you agree?" He sneered.

"I'm not alone, I have you," Linx sniggered cockily.

"You have quite the mouth on you for someone so young. How old are you? Is it twelve or thirteen? I always forget," Vladimir stepped a little closer as he said it, slowly backing the boy into a corner.

"I'm thirteen!" Linx snarled angrily, "Now tell me the news!"

"There was an attack earlier. Your mummy and daddy didn't survive. The reverend has evacuated the mountain for today whilst he investigates . . . Some sort of animal attack . . . I believe," his lips smirked as he said it.

Linx put the dots together quickly, "Only a vampire can kill a wolf!" He gasped.

"Dear child, you're forgetting that demons can kill anything . . . And being right next to the gates of Hell, I'd say that that's a logical assumption, wouldn't you agree?" He was almost in touching distance now as he took another slow step forward.

"YOU DID THIS!!!" Linx hissed.

"Lets not throw accusations around without proof," he leered.

"YOU'LL PAY FOR THIS!!!" Linx foamed at the mouth.

"Down boy!" Vladimir snickered, "I'm just here to collect you and take you to your dad's one gay brother and his partner, they'll be your new guardians now. Don't shoot the messenger," his untrustworthy lips smirked once more as he said it.

"I don't like you," Linx growled.

"A thirteen year old boy doesn't like me," Vladimir laughed, "I'm crushed."

"I know you're here to kill me, so just get on with it!" Linx felt tears enter his eyes.

"It's not very smart to taunt a Vampire," Vladimir grinned and licked his lips.

"And it's not very smart to corner a wolf!" Linx snarled.

Vladimir burst out in mocking-laughter, "You're not a wolf, you're the runt of the litter. Tell me child, what's a little pup like you doing working the mines?"

"My father thought I was strong enough and I've proved a good stone collector," Linx explained with a satisfied nod, but felt his eyes swell up with tears as he mentioned his father, "Are they really dead?"

"Yes little puppy. There is no wolf pack to protect you anymore," Vladimir was now in biting distance as his cold fishy breath blew against Linx's face, "The hilarious thing here is, you are not even a wolf and you don't even know it." The boy swallowed his nerves as he thought about his father and what he had taught him over the years.

"A wolf's strength comes from within, we don't need to be transitioned to defeat a vampire, nor do we need to hunt in packs," Linx threatened.

Vladimir was unfazed by the threat as he smiled and whispered, "Even if that were true child. It takes a fully grown adult to even stand a chance, and even if you did have that strength within you, you've spent the last eight hours working a hydraulic Jackhammer. I think I'll take my chances," his fangs now snarled a horror grin.

Linx quickly realised that the vampire was right. He was covered in grime and the sweat was dripping off of his face. His shirt was drenched and his breathing was still a little heavy. But there was no way he was going to go down without a fight. Linx with both hands shoved Vladimir hard in the chest.

"You just broke the truce!" His fangs foamed aggressively and angrily now as he leapt for Linx's neck.

Instinctively just like his father had taught him, he protected his neck by lifting his elbow, planting it onto the jaw of the vampire who's own momentum and eagerness sent him crashing into the cave wall.

Vladimir bounced off the wall and charged forward in a rage, but Linx had picked up the huge Jackhammer. He whacked the blood-sucker directly in the face which sent him crashing to the floor. Linx saw his chance to end this quickly as he rapidly plunged the tip head of the steel alloy drill deep into him, pinning the Vampire to the rocks. Linx now wished he hadn't burnt out the motor.

"AHHHHHHHHHH," Vladimir sighed as he yanked the drill free from within him as though he were plucking a splinter out, "If only it were a wooden stake and a little more to the left."

"Leave me alone!" Linx sobbed as he tried to run away. The vampire had leapt through the air now, pouncing onto Linx and knocking him to the floor as his mouth snarled with foaming dripping saliva. "You stupid little brat! Have you not been listening to my hints? You're not a Werewolf and never will be! And now you will die!"

Linx shut his eyes in terror as the fangs came down toward his neck.

"WHAT IS THIS?!!!!!!!!!!" The deep crusty voice of Reverend Crone boomed, echoing around the caves.

Vladimir leapt back and vanished into the shadows as quick as a flash – he was gone.

Linx felt a huge sigh of relief smother him. He leapt up and full of tears, he ran and hugged the priest tight.

"I'm sorry for your loss," the reverend comforted . . .

"That Vampire tried to break the truce and attack me. He's lucky I didn't kill him!" Linx raged.

"I have something to tell you young man," the Reverend said, "Although Werewolf blood flows through your ancestor's veins, and your fathers, it is not in you. Your grandfather wanted a normal life for his grandchildren. Part of the magic truce was that the wolf curse be lifted. The last proper Werewolf died when your father just died, and your uncle hasn't the strength, when your uncle eventually passes, the Werewolf's will be extinct."

"But that doesn't make sense! Why would my grandfather lift a curse that allows us to fight back against those monsters?" Linx sobbed.

The Reverend sighed. "Vladimir Putin and his son Lingwood are the only two left of their kind. The deal was that if we use enough stones to break the moon curse, then Vladimir and his son would remain inside the castle of Stadley Hold under the watchful eye of the headmaster. Vladimir wouldn't dare go up against the headmaster. Your grandfather saved the world from the horrors of Vladimir and Lingwood Putin. Myself and the headmaster will never let any harm come to you. So you and your brother are safe," the priest reassured. The thirteen year old boy dropped to his knees crying over his dad "I'm moving my brother out of this castle. I'm not having him live within the same walls as those monsters!"

"You took the stone chaser oath. You can't leave this castle Linx," the Reverend reminded.

"But my younger brother hasn't taken the oath yet. I'm getting him out of here," Linx said with determination.

"That will be down to your uncle," the Reverend asserted.

"NO! IT IS DOWN TO ME!" Linx raged and the Reverend smiled at his glare.

"Yes son, with fire in your belly like that, I believe it will be."

Linx stopped thinking back. Six years and the ache was still fresh, like a raw angry nerve. Vladimir had denied the cave incident, and The Reverend assumed it was a demon playing tricks on him. Nobody believed a thirteen year old boy who had just lost both his parents. Everybody put it down to grief, but this has never been about healing for Linx, he wasn't looking for closure. The headmaster had made him honour the truce with Vladimir, but now that monsters son has taken a liking to Eleni, and he wasn't sure how much longer he could honour this thin truce, not when in his opinion Vladimir already violated it six years prior.

6- ODD FEELINGS.

We all had a great time at the beach and now Johnny was dropping us off into town so that we could go clothes shopping to pick out dresses for the upcoming school dance. I was a little relieved when Johnny dropped us off and drove away, it had been forever since I had had a girlie night out, and the oestrogen rush was invigorating. We spoke mainly about boys as we walked to the one big department store in this dreary town.

"Thanks for jumping in and helping out at the beach," Sofia suddenly said to everyone, but she was looking at Jade as she said it. Something in Sofia's eyes told Jade that she was sorry for what she had said, and they exchanged a quiet nod and a smirk.

"So are you going to text Tom?" Jade asked Sofia, feeling like she should break the ice between them.

"No," she replied bewilderedly.

"Then why did you take his number?" I giggled.

"So that I can save it in my phone, so that if he somehow gets *my* number, I know not to answer it," she insisted smugly.

"He's cute," Stephanie blurted.

"You think every man is cute!" Sofia snapped.

"He is though," Estella agreed.

Sofia smirked, "He's alright. Nothing to shout home about."

"I think you like him," I insisted, "I caught a few smiles sent his way."

Sofia smirked.

"You do like him!" Dotty gasped.

"No I don't," Sofia denied.

Stephanie jabbered on trying to get her to confess, but I interrupted with a question about dresses, to spare her. Sofia threw a grateful glance my way.

The dance was supposedly semiformal, but none of us really understood exactly what that meant. All the girls seemed surprised that I had never been to a dance before as they all shot me disbelieving looks.

"You never went with a boyfriend or anything, not ever?" Stephanie questioned dubiously as we sauntered through the front doors of the store.

"I never got asked," I shrugged, "I've never had a boyfriend or anything remotely close," I confessed.

"Why?" Stephanie demanded.

"I don't know," I replied sheepishly.

"Well what about luscious Lingwood?" Jade fluttered her eyelashes.

"I'm so jealous," Stephanie snickered.

"You have Johnny," Estella reminded her.

"Yeah, but Johnny is like a Reno Megane and Lingwood is a goddamn Ferrari," she purred, "I'd trade that in for an upgrade."

"What about Linx?" Sofia snorted.

"He's a Lamborghini," Stephanie bit her lip seductively as she said it.

I was gobsmacked that I thought about his younger brother taking me for a ride in his Lambo once he had fixed it up. Not that I know anything about cars, but a Lamborghini is awesome! I gulped the thought back down and put it down to the excitement of going for a spin in such a car. Not anything to do with him liking me! And certainly nothing to do with me liking him! Because I don't! But I couldn't deny the warm feeling of being in his happy company. His friendliness, pure positivity and smiley face was addictive. I closed my eyes for a second and all I could see was his beautiful beaming joyful grin. *GO AWAY!* I shouted inside my head. I was terrified that I was going to start liking three men at once, and this would be too much to handle. He was far too young for me and besides I liked his older brother who wasn't interested in me for the same reasons I'm not interested in Harry, the age gap! The irony wasn't lost on me. But luscious Lingwood *is* interested in me, at least I think he is, and he is intoxicatingly gorgeous . . . But he might be a vampire!

"And what do you know about cars?" Estella laughed.

"She's been in the back seats of many," Sofia sniggered.

"You've ridden in many cars?" Dotty said innocently.

Sofia shot her a perplexed glare.

"I don't think Sofia meant that sort of ride, Dotty," Jade snickered.

"Shut up!" Stephanie chuckled, "I'm not *that* bad!"

"Oh," Dotty gasped.

We all giggled as we entered the junior section.

"What about Harry?" Stephanie smirked, "I saw you two walking off down the beach together."

"We're just friends," I explained as we began to scan the racks for dress-up clothes as we spoke. "Besides, he's too young, he's just a boy!"

"Yeah experience is a good thing, but the younger they are the more passionate they are," Stephanie poked her tongue out.

"I think two men are enough for one girl," Estella laughed.

"Yeah but he's not a man," Sofia gibed.

"Eleni will make him a man," Jade joined in.

"Two and a half men," Dotty cackled, "I love that show."

"You guys are terrible!" I sighed, "I don't have *two* men, and I'm certainly not interested in that boy."

We all giggled as we found the dress racks. Now we had work to do!

"Who are you trying to convince, us? Or yourself?" Stephanie snickered as she pawed through the clothes.

I ground my teeth, "Trust me! Linx isn't interested in me and his younger brother is far too young, and as for Lingwood, I'm unsure."

"What are you unsure of?" Stephanie giggled.

"He blows hot and cold with me," I confessed.

"You going to be *blowing* with him too," Sofia laughed as she made a rude hand gesture to her mouth.

"Ewwwwww," I giggled.

"Is that how you are going to thank Tom for sticking up for you at the pools?" Jade laughed, and Sofia stuck her tongue out pretending to gag.

"Boys and their games!" Stephanie groaned with an eye roll, "You have to turn the tables, act like you are not interested."

"I don't think *you* should be the one to give advice on playing hard to get," Sofia giggled.

"Yeah you're the expert on that one Sofia!" Stephanie snapped, "Are you ever going to text Tom?"

Sofia sighed as she picked up some clothes. The dress selection wasn't large, but we all managed to try a few things on and soon found the perfect dresses for us and the perfect shoes. Jade found a beautiful knee-length pink skater dress with spaghetti straps. Dotty, after we made her put down the jeans and an ACDC T-shirt, chose a long strapless, basic black dress. Stephanie was caught between an electric blue dress that matched her eyes, and a green dress that draped around her tall frame nicely, making her hair look even more fiery red. We critiqued and felt the green dress made her look like Poison Ivy from Batman, so she went along with her first choice of blue, but then decided it didn't show enough cleavage! – So she went with a strapless tight-fitting red dress and a huge push-up bra to make her look like she had assets that she actually didn't have. Although to her credit, her pale skin and stunning blue eyes and flowing red hair against the blood-red dress, really stood out in a good way.

"Do you think this dress is short enough?" Stephanie asked as she looked at it. It went all the way down to her ankle but had a split to show the leg.

"Leave something to the imagination, will you," Sofia groaned, "You can see your whole leg anyway, almost your knickers!"

Stephanie smiled as she admired herself in the mirror.

Estella then came out the dressing room clad in a nice blue pencil skirt and a white long sleeved top to match her beautiful white heels.

"Do these red heels make me too tall?" Stephanie asked.

"You'll end up on your back anyway, what's it matter?" Sofia grumbled.

Stephanie frowned, "Maybe I'll get to know Tom."

"Maybe I'll cut off all your hair tonight whilst you sleep," Sofia said eerily.

Stephanie gulped.

I chose a black dress but the girls made me put it back, saying that with my short-ish black hair, I didn't look right in a black dress. I reluctantly agreed with them as I tried on my second choice – A silver Maxi-dress that sparkled. I wasn't completely sure, but the girls convinced me that I had to get it. I slipped my foot into some white-heels that Stephanie talked me into wearing. I had never worn heals before and almost took a tumble inside the shop.

Sofia was the only one who hadn't come out the changing room.

"Are you alright?" I called in as I gently knocked on the door.

"I'm fine. I'm not sure why I am trying on dresses anyway. I'm more of a jeans and jumper kinda girl!" Sofia sighed frustratingly.

"Just open the door!" I demanded.

She slowly and reluctantly slid the door slightly and poked her head out.

"I'm wearing a dress," she announced, looking horrified.

"Well, that is different from your usual black jeans and jumpers with your Bomber Jacket and Converse," I joked, "Are you going to keep me in suspense?"

"I used to wear jumper and T-shirt-dresses back when I had hair," she confessed miserably, "I actually prefer Jumpers, jean-shorts and pulled up socks with boots."

"Oh really?" I tried to hide my complete shock and surprise.

"Yes, and if I'm really dressing up then I have gold hoop earrings and a Black Animal Print Puff A-Line Dress, with black biker boots, in my wardrobe at home," she said with an unhappy smile.

"How does not having hair stop you from wearing those clothes now?" I asked with pity, "I saw your body at the beach when we went in the pool. You have an amazing body, why hide it?"

"Because I'm not a slut that needs to show off anything!" She growled.

"But you said you used to wear Jean-shorts and T-shirt-dresses," I challenged her, "It doesn't make you a slut!"

"It's hardly showing my body off," Sofia argued, "Besides, it's not like you're one to talk! You are probably the plainest person on the planet!"

"I imagine it would have shown your fantastic legs and arse. Certainly better than jeans and jumpers all the time," I pointed out, ignoring her dig at me. I was starting to realise that Sofia's hard and mean shell was clearly a defensive tactic, designed to protect her true feelings and insecurities.

"I'm barely five-foot-four-inches, honey. I certainly don't have great legs," Sofia disagreed.

"Your body is toned and gorgeous. I saw it at the beach!" I reminded her. "I've never seen you this vulnerable. You weren't yourself at the beach and you aren't now. Where is tough Sofia? What have you done with my friend?" I joked.

"Shut up! Tell me what you think and then leave me alone!" Sofia grumbled as she finally opened the door fully, revealing her entire outfit.

My eyes bulged from my head.

"I think you look stunning!" I complimented.

Sofia tried to hide the sad smirk and tears in her eyes.

It was a purple Sequin High Neck mini dress with the most incredible curly silver and different shades of purple pattern swimming through it like waves. She was taller thanks to the lace up black platform heels, - and she looked sensational. Suddenly Dotty popped her head round the corner.

"Oh my god, you look, you look . . . AMAZING!" She drooled. Sofia held her head up high and her moment of vulnerability had passed. I smiled as I now saw straight through the tough-girl act as she strutted out of the changing rooms as though she owned the place. Stephanie's jaw dropped and hit the floor when she saw Sofia. Estella was speechless too.

"Wow!" Jade gasped.

"Where you been hiding that figure girl?" Estella asked.

"If I wore that then you'd call me a slut," Stephanie moaned.

"You are a slut," Sofia said with a smile.

Stephanie frowned and looked a little upset.

"But you're my friend, and you look amazing in your outfit," Sofia surprised everyone with *that* compliment.

"Wait, did you just compliment me? Or am I dreaming?" Stephanie gasped sarcastically.

"She complimented you," Estella clarified with an equal sound of surprise to her voice.

We all glared at her speechless.

Sofia frowned, "What you all gawking at?"

"Tom is a lucky guy," Dotty lusted.

Sofia rolled her eyes, "I'm going to the dance alone," she insisted.

"Well, looking like *that* you're going to steal the show," Jade said.

"Everyone is looking at you," Estella whispered.

Sofia frowned and looked around, and they were.

"It's because you look fantastic," Stephanie returned the compliment.

Sofia nodded, "I know," she said confidently as she turned on her heal and strutted back into the changing rooms. When she re-emerged in her jumper and jeans, it was almost like it wasn't the same girl.

"Let's pay for these and go get some grub," she suggested as she marched past us.

"I want to look for some jewellery first," Stephanie insisted.

"Me too," Estella and Jade both agreed.

Sofia nodded.

"I'm going to go and try and find a book shop. Meet you back here?" I suggested.

"No," Sofia replied. "Meet us at 'The Italian' restaurant down the road at 6pm."

I looked at my watch and it said 5pm.

"Ok," I said as I wondered off.

Dotty chased after me, "Take a right as you come out of here and there are some book shops just up the road, just remember to keep heading downtown," she pointed out.

"Thanks," I said as I followed her instructions.

I had no trouble finding the book shop, but it was not what I was looking for. The windows were dusty and full of some sort of crystals and dream catchers and lots of various different supernatural based novels and spiritual healing guides. So I decided I'd call that one a miss. I could just about make out through the glass, an old lady with a welcoming expression written across her features. She had long curly white hair and looked as though she was a little *too* friendly. I immediately found myself thinking of the Witch in Hansel and Gretel that seemed so welcoming, before she tried to cook the children! I then spotted a book about horses and immediately felt a lump in my throat at the thought of my beloved Fiona. I was almost tempted to go inside once I saw that book. It was an attracting enticement, but then I found my mind thinking of the tempting candy, cake, pastries and gingerbread that lured the children into that cannibalistic witch's house. I knew I was being silly as it was just a fairytale, but my mind had done enough to freak me out, especially when we were right on Hells doorstep . . . literally. So I moved on down the road. There had to be a normal book shop in town somewhere.

I meandered through the cobbled streets. The roads were beginning to get a bit busy, filling up with townsfolk that I guessed had just finished work. I suppose this was this small town's rush-hour, I assumed as the end-of-workday traffic gathered. I hoped I was heading downtown like Dotty had said. I stupidly wasn't paying as much attention as to where I was walking and heading, as I should had been. My pathetic pitiful mind was going over Lingwood and Lynx and what Harry had said about Vampires and Werewolves – among other things. Not to mention my anxiety about the upcoming dance, I was constantly wrestling with despair and now I was a little lost. I stomped along in what I think was a south-ish-sort of direction, toward some glass-window-fronted-shops. These looked hopeful. But when I got to them the promising shops were a major disappointment. It was just a repair shop and a sweetshop. I ran my fingers across my scalp, brushing through my hair a couple of times and taking some huge gulps of air. My chest rose high and plummeted down as I took the deep breaths before I continued around the dark corner. I soon realised after crossing several roads that I was heading in the complete wrong direction. All the traffic seemed to be heading in the other direction and this area of town seemed a little abandoned. I passed warehouse after warehouse before I came to my senses and realised I should probably go back, so I twisted east . . . I think. As I took a turn at the next corner I mapped it out in my head that if I looped back around, then I should be on a different street where there may be a bookstore of some sorts. Plus I should also be heading roughly in the right direction back to the boardwalk. – I hoped!

Suddenly a group of men strolled around the corner and were heading my way. There were four of them and they seemed too causally dressed to be heading home from work, I assumed, yet too grubby-looking to be tourists. As they got closer I realised that they must be similar ages to me, maybe slightly older, early twenties perhaps. They were fooling around and joking loudly among themselves. Chuckling hoarsely and playfully punching each other on the arms, shoulders and groin region. They were just a typical bunch of lads laughing raucously, as men tend to do when they're in their packs, messing around and acting bolshy. I swiftly changed the direction of my walk to as far over near the wall as I could, to allow the grimy-looking group to pass by with plenty of space. I focused my glare on the pavement as I daren't make eye-contact, as I scooted my butt rapidly past them.

"Hello-hello!" One of them called out to me as I rushed past them.

Another then wolf-whistled.

I glanced over my shoulder automatically to double check they weren't talking to someone else, but that was me just being stupid. Of course they were talking to me, there was nobody else around! Suddenly I realised that only two had passed me and my heart stopped. Two of them had paused in front of me and the other two behind me were slowing down, trapping me between them.

"Excuse me," I mumbled, a knee-jerk reaction as I quickly crossed the road to escape.

"Where you going, sweetheart?" One of them yelled, "What's the hurry?"

I quickly looked away and upped my speed-walk towards the corner. I could hear their laughter at full volume behind me. "Hey, wait!" I heard one of them call out to me.

I kept my head down and walked even faster through the gears - almost a dash at this point, as I twisted the corner and out of sight. I leaned against the wall for a second and breathed a sigh of relief as my heart thumped a rock concert in my chest. I could still hear them chortling and knew I had better keep going.

This area was empty now. The small pathway next to the huge warehouses spiralled off into almost nothing as there was nothing but plant life and dusty grey sand. I turned another corner and now I was confronted by row after row of huge warehouses again. They were grave-coloured each with huge bay doors for unloading big vehicles like Lorries. I searched for some people - a trucker, a worker, anyone, but everything seemed padlocked up for the night. The other side of the street had no path now, only a chain-link fence topped with barbed wire. It was some sort of junk yard that it was protecting, full of car parts and god-knows-what other scrap. It looked at a glance like it could be engine parts or something. Not that I'd have a clue. I think I was heading towards the port, as I had wondered too far. I doubt any tourist was meant to see this part of town.

The weather begun to close in and it was getting dark and cold. The clouds were piling up on the horizon, causing the skies to grey with streaks of pink and orange. The bad weather was giving the illusion of an early sunset and real chill crept into the air. I'd stupidly left my jacket in Johnny's minivan. Just as I thought that, just out of pure coincidence, a van similar to Johnny's minivan shot past me. Its headlights startled me for a second and in a brief glorious moment of hope, I thought that salvation had arrived; I thought it was Johnny and the girls coming to rescue me. I soon realised it wasn't him and a cold shiver made me cross my arms to my chest as my breath danced in front of me. Now the road was empty.

The sky all of a sudden blackened further as the dark clouds swooped in rapidly. I twisted my neck to glance over my shoulder to set my eyes upon the offending storm that was approaching fast, when something caught my eye and alarm bells started ringing. I realised with utter horror and shock that two men were walking silently roughly-twenty-feet behind me.

They were from the same grimy group of lads I had passed earlier on. My heart sank and I turned my head, quickening my walk. A coldness that had nothing to do with the weather embraced me. I shivered as the chill worked its way down my spine. *What do they want?* – I fretted.

My handbag was dangling over my shoulder and I thought about slinging the strap across my body to prevent them from snatching it easily. But then I changed my mind as I thought I could perhaps use it to swing at them like a weapon. Not that it would do much. I knew exactly where my pepper spray was – not here! I could have screamed at my stupidity of not even unpacking it from my duffle bag that was shoved under my bed in Stadley Hold. I barely had any money on me, perhaps a few twenties. I considered *accidently* dropping my purse and then running away. – But then my throat became dry and I became hot and sweaty. A small voice in the back of my mind warned me and asked me the dreaded question – *what if they are something worse than just bag-snatchers?* I gulped as I realised that if they had wanted to snatch my bag, then why didn't they try when I passed them earlier? Now I was adamant that they were worse than just thieves. The adrenalin and fear fought around my body. I listened intently to their silent footsteps, which were much too quiet. Especially when I compared it to the rowdy racket they'd been making earlier when I passed them. The boisterous lads seemed eerily quiet now as they walked. It was creepy! But they didn't appear to be speeding up, or gaining on me. In fact they seemed as though they were just strolling. *Breathe* – I spoke to myself. *They might have just said bye to their mates and now are walking home* – I reminded myself – *home that so-happens to be coincidently in the same exact direction as me* – I gulped. I wasn't fully convinced that they were following me, although it did seem strange. I continued to walk at a fast pace, gaining momentum with each step, going as fast as I possibly could without running and making it too obvious. They didn't appear to be getting closer to me. I focused my mind on the turning that was coming up ahead, as my feet skipped across the floor at speed, I was caught somewhere between a power-walk and a jog, although I wanted to break out into a full-blown-sprint and just get to safety!

The turning was only a few yards from me now and I could hear them, staying as far back as they could. I kept trying to convince myself that I wasn't being pursued and that it was all in my imagination. I let out a gigantic sigh of relief as I turned the corner. Then my heart froze inside my chest as it sank to the pit of my stomach. My eyes bulged and tears of terror seeped from them. The turning was a dead end!

I could hear their faint footsteps getting nearer now.

I hastily gazed across the street. There was no way out! Panic-stricken, I looked left towards the men that were still heading my way. They were still a fair distance back, but they were staring right at me. I turned my head right and looked on ahead. The buildings bridged together more and more as the street narrowed, until finally the buildings met, putting an end to the street.

My breathe hitched as a panic attack begun.

All of a sudden a little dim pink-purple glow appeared down the street where the houses met. It was no bigger than a tennis ball. It hovered around and sparkled and then vanished down a gap between the buildings.

My heart rose from my chest and I almost choked with relief. There was an alleyway that lead in-between the two warehouses and onto another street. I dashed instantly up the road. It seemed to take me forever to get to the gap. I glanced back at the two men and with each step I took they seemed to fall further behind - to my great relief. They were roughly forty yards back now as I finally reached the alleyway, but their eyes were still locked on me. I calmly walked into the alleyway until they were out of sight, then I ran! I run faster than I had ever ran before, until I reached the end of the dark alleyway, darting out onto the street. It was another empty street! Where was everybody? – I panicked, but then spotted some cars up the street and a few people. I exhaled with relief. I skipped around the corner in the direction that the cars went, with a grateful sigh. Then skidded to an abrupt halt. The street was lined on both sides with just brickwork, almost like a giant alleyway. There was a street light flickering on and off and the other two were broken - making this street the scariest one yet. I could see in the faint distance about two streets ahead, a group of people talking and cars. They were lit up by streetlights too. I gulped as I looked upon the blank, doorless, windowless walls that were either side of this street. I had to get to those people, I had to just get through this last street and then there would be too many people and bright lights and

I'd be safe. – But then my heart sank to the pit of my stomach and my body went arctic cold with terror. The people were too far away! Because lounging against one of the buildings, midway down the darkened street, were the other two men from the boisterous group. They were both watching me with excited smiles. Suddenly I could hear those faint footsteps behind me again and the horror hit me head on like a train. I wasn't being chased, followed, or pursued. I was being herded!!! I was frozen like a statue as they closed in on me from both sides. I quickly crossed the street, but I knew it was a wasted attempt at prolonging the inevitable. I had the worse sinking feeling imaginable as I daren't look back. I scrapped my hands pathetically against the brick wall, as if I was trying to climb it. But they had me cornered.

"There you are darling," one of their booming voices shattered the intense quiet and scorched my ears, making me jump.

"Oh shit," I wheezed with anxiety as I paused for a second, but it felt like a very long time. I had a good loud scream, and I sucked in air, preparing to use it, but I instantly coughed. My throat was rough and horse. The fear had stolen my volume and my dry throat now protested with pain.

I warily and slowly turned around.

"Stay away from me!" I tried to sound threatening with the warning, but I sounded more like a squeaky mouse as the apprehension stole any conviction and volume. I gripped my purse tightly, ready to either surrender it, or use it as some sort of weapon.

"What's a nice girl like you doing all alone out here?" One asked.

"Leave me alone," I pleaded and begged.

"Don't be like that, baby," one of the men said, and then that awful raucous laughter from them all begun again.

I was backed right up against the wall now as they swarmed in like predators about to get their prey. I braced myself, feet apart, trying to remember through my blind panic all the sparring lessons with Linx that I had had. – *BLANK!* My mind went fucking blank!!! All those self defence classes and fighting classes with Linx had been a waste of time. Tears now escaped my eyes as one of them said the dreaded words that I feared most. The words that summed it all up in a nutshell and confirmed my worst fears that they were not interested in robbing me. "We are going to show you a *real* good time, darling."

I gulped loudly and I knew I was like a deer caught in headlights as terror seized control of my body, rendering me speechless and motionless. I was completely incapacitated and helpless. I knew that even if I did remember anything that Linx had taught me with self-defence, there was four of them and only one of me. I didn't stand a chance!

Suddenly, that glowing ball reappeared in a blinding flash of iridescent whites and glows of purple. We all squinted and shielded our eyes as the harsh light erupted. Then it suddenly stopped. I peeked out from behind my forearm and could see a woman standing in the street. She had a Lilac lace-skin-tight bodice, colour-coded with various different shades of light-violets and a floating ghostly-faded-amethyst-purple tight dress that licked the floor, embroidered with flowers dappled with many shades of blanched lavender. The glow around her was ablaze as a riot of different purples bleached the atmosphere. Everything outside of her glow seemed bleak, gloomy and sombre. Her eyes shun a bold purple and very bright, clear, and were deep dark and strong in colour against her delicate pleasant pale-white-snow-skin. Her brilliant, vivid and intense unicorn pastel hair swirled in the wind around her.

Indira was here . . .

Her electric bright and metallic glowing eyes locked onto the men in front of me.

Their face's after their eyes had adjusted to the various harmonious shades of light purple that lit up the street, looked discoloured.

She held out her fluorescent ice-coloured hand with her flamboyant faded-plum-coloured manicured Purple Ombre nails. Her skin was almost glistening and sparkling like shining glitter, under the moonlight that seeped through the clouds and onto her.

Indira's autumn burnt-sepia-red lips smiled when she saw me. They were mellow, soft and pure in colour.

It was amazing how instantaneously the choking fear vanished as soon as she smiled at me, and how the sudden feeling of security scooped me up.

"Wow," the men gasped with pure terrified lust in their eyes. Indira's prismatic and psychedelic dark eyelashes flickered as her opalescent pastel eyes shot back towards them.

"Are you an angel?" One gasped.

Indira's vibrant smile widened as she blew them a kiss. – Purple mist sprinkled from her hand and onto them. She then reached her hand out to me. I immediately placed my warm sweaty palm inside her perfect lithe and manicured grip – and suddenly we were someplace else – a different street.

I stared at her face in profound relief, relief that went beyond my sudden deliverance. I studied her flawless features as I tried to get my breathing back to normal.

"Did we just teleport?" I gasped, as my heart still thumped hard within my chest, causing me to act as though I had just tried to break the world record for breath-holding.

"Walk with me," she insisted, ignoring my question, "You're safe now," And with that my breathing finally calmed.

"What was that purple mist you sprinkled those creeps with?" I asked as I walked next to her.

Indira's wonderful rare-forest-bird laughter was the most beautiful sound I had ever heard.

"The pulsing you feel in your wrist when you are late for class. They're now going to feel that same pulsing every time they have a sinful thought, except it won't be in their wrists," she glanced down at my crotch.

"Brilliant!" I beamed and we both continued to laugh.

"So, Eleni, I wanted to make good on that promise from the other day that I'd come and find you. So that we can discuss the element sword that called out to you," Indira's soft voice spoke.

"The Time Peer of the realm sword," I replied.

She stopped and turned to look at me. "Yes. What do you know of it?"

"I know that it can only be wielded by 'Time Aristocrat's' and they don't exist anymore," I said.

"Until now," Indira corrected me, as she looked right at me with those piercing mauve eyes.

"W-w-what?" I stuttered.

"I knew I sensed extreme power within you when you spotted that demon possessing Reverend Crone. To be able to see a demon takes great strength. If you think of all the people in that room, powerful people, it was *you* that spotted it. Not any of us," she admitted.

"But I'm just a Stone-Chaser," I said with a frown.

"Oh Eleni. In a male-occupied world, we felines can't afford to sell ourselves short. Especially when born with such a gift," Indira placed her hands to my cheeks and pinched slightly.

"It can't be a gift if that sort of magic is banished," I pointed out.

Her facial expression hardened and her eyebrows stooped with deep thought as though she had just figured something out.

"Time Aristocrat," she mumbled to herself in a whisper. "That would explain why Jealousaw saw you."

My body suddenly went cold with dread, "So, he *did* spot me?" I asked, and was surprised at how hoarse my voice sounded.

"It would appear so, yes," her voice sounded livid.

"What does this mean?" I gulped.

She backed away slightly. Her expression seemed almost murderously angry, an expression I didn't think I'd ever see from her aw-so-perfect face, but even angry she looked so pretty.

"Are you ok?" I asked as I tried to cough away my rough throat.

"No," she said curtly, and her tone sounded as though she was going to burst into tears. "You just reminded me of someone - for a second there - that I used to know. That's all."

"Who?" I asked.

"Nobody of importance," she said with a friendly smile, "Let's get you back to your friends, shell we?"

"But I thought you were going to discuss the sword with me?" I asked, trying not to sound too upset.

She exhaled deeply. "Are you hungry?"

"Yes, starving," I chuckled as I looked at my watch. It was past 6pm and I knew the girls would be worried about me. Indira almost as though she had read my mind, grabbed my hand quickly and suddenly we were outside the Italian restaurant where my friends were. Sofia, Jade, Dotty, Stephanie and Estella were all just leaving the restaurant.

"Hey!" I shouted as I called after them.

They rushed over to me, the pronounced relief on all their faces simultaneously changing to lust mixed with shock as they saw Indira. A reaction she seemed to often provoke from people due to her glowing goddess like grace.

They stopped in their tracks and hesitated a few feet from me.

"Are you ok?" Jade blurted.

And before I could answer her Sofia jumped in, "Where have you been?" She said suspiciously.

"You missed a lovely dinner," Dotty grinned whilst licking her lips.

Suddenly Indira spoke, her soft silken voice drifted sweetly into our ears, "Would you mind if I took Eleni for dinner?"

I could tell by their staggered expressions that Indira's irresistible lullaby voice had the exact same affect on them that it had on me. Every time she spoke it was like you were enchanted and spellbound as her words trickled into your ear canals like warm honey.

Stephanie was the first to speak as the other girls seemed a little perplexed, "Sure, we don't mind," she spoke slowly as she bit her lip.

The other girls broke from their dumbstruck daze and agreed. "See you later Eleni. Bye Miss Amitola," and they trotted off.

"I must apologise," I said sheepishly to her after the girls had left.

Indira turned to me and seemed confused, "What for, sweet child?"

"I've been calling you Indira all this time when out of respect for you being a teacher, I should be referring to you as Miss Amitola," I prattled on, "Which is a beautiful name by the way."

"Thank you, Eleni. My actual full name is Indira Evelina Amitola. But you can call me *just* Indira, if you like?" She smiled sweetly upon me.

Is it possible to fall in love with a name? I pondered as I held the door open for her.

The restaurant wasn't crowded - the host was female, not that it would have mattered, as she had this affect on both genders anyway. I immediately understood the look in her eyes as she assessed Indira. It was the same look we all had in her presence, and I was beginning to wonder if Indira had deliberately put us all under the same covetousness spell. She welcomed Indira a little more warmly than necessary. I was absolutely horrified and shocked at how much this actually bothered me. The host was quite a bit taller than I was, and she clearly over-bleached her hair, as it was so unnaturally blonde it made me squint. The tall fake-blonde-bimbo went to ask the obvious next question, but Indira was quicker.

"Just the two of us," Indira's voice was alluring, and I still couldn't work out if she knew exactly what she was doing and the affect that she had on the people around her.

I spotted the woman's eyes flicker to me and then quickly away, clearly satisfied by my ugliness and just plain ordinariness. I couldn't help but have my claws out ready to pounce. I'm not usually catty or jealous and I was quite astounded by my sudden urge to claw her eyes out. I frowned down at the floor and banished those ridiculous thoughts. This woman was just being friendly, perhaps a little overly friendly, but nonetheless it's not her fault that Indira has this intoxicating magnetic pull that surrounds her. The tall yellowhead led us to a table in the middle of the room. There were a few seats nearby with a fair amount of people sitting and eating and we seemed a little crammed in. I was about to sit at the table that was offered, when Indira's lovely voice flooded my ears.

"Please could we have something a little more private," she whispered politely to the host.

"Of course," the woman replied quickly. She turned and led us around a wall with pretty lights and decorations on, to a small ring of booths that were empty and out the way.

"Is this suitable?"

"Perfect," Indira flashed her gleaming smile, dazing her for a moment.

"Um," the host shook her head, blinking and blushing, "Your server will be out momentarily," she walked away unsteadily.

"Do you have any idea the affect you have on everyone?" I sniggered.

Indira's mesmerizing glowing Mauve eyes, shun almost Indigo, as she gazed upon me with a confused expression, "Affect?"

"Yes, you dazzle them. That woman is probably hyperventilating in the kitchen right now," I chuckled.

She seemed confused. She tilted her head to one side and her eyes seemed curious, "I dazzle people?"

I looked at her dubiously for a second, but her childlike innocence caught me off guard - her butter-wouldn't-melt facial expressions unhinged me.

"Never mind," I blushed as I glanced away a little embarrassed.

"Do I dazzle you?"

"Yes, frequently!" I reluctantly admitted as I couldn't bring myself to meet her stunning gaze.

The fact that she seemed oblivious to it made her even more enticing. Or was that on purpose too? I was relieved that our waitress suddenly appeared, saving me from awkwardness. The brunettes face was expectant. The hostess had obviously said something about Indira, dishing out the details behind the scenes. The pretty brunette didn't look disappointed as her eyes lit up at the sight of this enchanting goddess that sat opposite me.

"Oh my god, you are so beautiful," the waitress complimented in her Italian accent.

"Do I dazzle you?" Indira asked the waitress, smirking. Indira's eyes, that had entrapped the poor waitress like headlights would a deer, quickly flickered to me and then back to the waitress. I then thought back to her sexual banter with Reverend Crone and remembered that Indira had a very good sense-of-humour, when she felt playful. The waitress to her credit, kept composed, although I could see in her eyes that her heart was fluttering.

"You do," she replied as she flipped a strand of her dark brown hair behind one of her ears and smiled with unnecessary warmth. I tried not to roll my eyes.

"My name is Annamaria, and I'll be your waitress for tonight. Can I get you anything to drink?" I didn't miss the fact that Annamaria hadn't looked my way, not even once. She was only speaking to Indira.

"I'll have a coke!" I piped up. I immediately regretted my outburst as I felt rude jumping ahead of Indira, but I wanted this waitress to at least acknowledge that I was here too. She nodded and noted it down, but still to my irritation didn't look my way. Her eyes were fixated on Indira, but Indira now looked at me.

"I'll have the same, please."

"I'll be right back with that," she assured Indira with another needless seductive smile. But Indira didn't see it. She was watching me. I felt as though Indira was trying to read my mind as her gaze scanned my face. I suddenly got butterflies in my stomach. What was wrong with me? I'm straight! I'm not gay! I'm not a lesbian. But I found myself wanting to explore Indira in so many more ways than my mind could comprehend. This bothered me - as I only felt this way when in her presence. I've never once looked at a woman in that way. Sure, I can appreciate someone who is pretty and attractive, but this was different. I was stuttering my words; I was mesmerised by her looks. I was, I was . . . possibly in love?

"It's been quite a troublesome night for you, hasn't it? How are you feeling?" Indira suddenly asked me.

"I'm ok," I replied, surprised by her intensity as her eyes stayed fixated on my face.

"You're not feeling sick, dizzy, or cold . . .?"

"Nope."

Indira smirked.

"That's good," she said, "It means you're not going into shock. Most people it can take a while to sink in, especially after a traumatic event such as tonight. You do understand what happened right?"

"I nearly got raped and *you* saved me, my knight in shining armour, *my* hero," I suddenly gritted my teeth and wanted to slap myself at saying all that. I must sound pathetic!

"That's good, you're not in denial. This is a good thing. – And, the term would be dame-in-shining-armour, not Knight," she corrected with a smile.

Suddenly as if on cue, the tears snuck up on me.

"Thank you," I sobbed.

Indira's beautiful smile glistened wider. "And the penny finally drops. Let's get some food and sugar inside you and you'll feel better," she insisted kindly and at that exact moment, as if Indira had somehow mind controlled the waitress; she promptly appeared with our drinks and a basket of breadsticks. The bitch stood with her back to me as she placed them on the table – apparently even when bawling my eyes out, I still didn't exist to this waitress.

"Are you ready to order?" She asked Indira.

"Eleni?" Indira asked and the waitress turned unwillingly towards me.

"The pasta," I said after I could breathe again, pointing to it on the menu.

She barely even acknowledged me as she shifted her body back towards Indira. "And for you?" She smiled, her eyes seemed star-struck, like a moth glaring towards a flame.

"Nothing for me, please," Indira insisted.

"Let me know if you change your mind," the waitress said as she finally broke away from her lustful stare. Indira's gaze was locked on me with a coy smile though, and the waitress left dissatisfied.

"I think that waitress has the hots for you," I giggled.

"Do I dazzle," Indira said playfully as she flicked her quicksilver-blue cascade of her unicorn lilac pastels and mystical silky mane, out of her face. Her curls caught the light as she flicked it and it was as if it were changing colour right before my very eyes. Waves of silver and hues of a blushing sky tinted the length of tresses, combined with winter wrapped around spring like a violet morning, as though feathers had been dipped in amaranthine ink. Changing constantly, - cascading mystical waves of sunrise with pale pastels in the hues of abalone - to a dusty-grey violet, or, a waterfall capturing sunset. It was like a purple-stripped sea nettle Jellyfish and quite possibly the most mystical and enchanting thing I have ever witnessed – the bleached-Mauve Orchid flame of her revolutionizing long hair, swirling around her shoulders.

I had wanted to make a joke or at least agree with her and confirm that she does dazzle, but instead my chin hit the table and I just knew that I went as red as a tomato.

Indira laughed playfully.

"Drink!" She ordered.

I sipped at my coke obediently, and then gulped the rest down. I was surprised at how thirsty I actually was as I guzzled it down. I didn't stop to even think that it sounded like rain gushing down a drainpipe. Suddenly I realised I had already finished the entire glass – and Indira slid her coke towards me.

"This is your drink," I protested.

"Sweet child. I got it for you," she said softly.

"Thanks," I muttered, still gasping for more. The cold from the icy drink was radiating through my chest and I couldn't help but shiver.

"Drink slower or you'll get cold," Indira warned - and at that exact moment that she said it, as though she had somehow known, I suddenly got brain-freeze.

Before I had even a chance to shake it off, Indira had wrapped a cardigan – that I didn't even know she had - around my shoulders.

It smelled incredible. I inhaled, trying to recognize the delicious scent, but I couldn't identify it. It didn't smell like perfume.

"That cardigan suits you Eleni," she complimented as her eyes watched me. I looked down, flushing, to my annoyance.

She then pushed the bread basket towards me.

"So, what did you want to talk with me about then?" I finally built up the courage to ask as I picked up a breadstick and started nibbling the end – "The time-sword-thingy?" I spoke with my mouthful.

"Yes, 'The Time Peer of the Realm Sword' is a bit of a mouthful, isn't it?" She chuckled her wonderful rare-forest-bird enchanting laugh. "A lot of secret and hidden artefacts refer to it as 'The Sword of Time.' It is a little easier to remember, too," she elucidated.

"So what has this got to do with me?" I asked.

Suddenly Indira looked displeased. Her pastel-purple-haze-almost-alabaster-eyebrows furrowed.

"This is much more complicated than I had anticipated," she murmured.

"I have a right to know," I mumbled in retaliation.

With that her expression changed back to warmth, "Of course you do sweet child. Let's start with what a 'Time Aristocrat' actually is."

"Thank you," I said as I chewed on the end of the breadstick, trying to look indifferent.

She took a breath, "Time Aristocrats' were hunted down and destroyed by Reverend Crone and your father," she looked sad as she said this.

My eyes narrowed, "WHAT? WHY?" I said a little loudly.

"Time-power is a forbidden power that very few wizards, witches and sorcerers have ever managed to wield. To be able to go back in time and change the past and influence the future, was a power considered too dangerous to exercise. The last remaining 'Time Aristocrat' is 'The Burned Soul' but due to all the 'Time-Swords' being destroyed, all except one. – Meant that the time magic is impossible to manipulate, even for someone as powerful as 'The Burned Soul'." She explained.

"But 'The Time Swords' are not all destroyed. Why leave one?" I asked.

"Because *that* sword was too powerful to destroy. We tried," Indira shrugged.

"What makes that sword different from the rest?" My interest was well and truly piqued now.

Indira looked as though she was worried suddenly,

"It belonged to *him*," she gulped.

"Who?" And with that the waitress strode across the partition with my pasta – eyes locked onto Indira. I suddenly realised we'd been instinctively leaning toward each other across the table, because we both quickly straightened up as she approached. She plonked the dish down in front of me and turned straight to Indira.

"Are you certain you don't want anything?" She asked, "Is there nothing I can offer you?" I may have been imagining the double meaning in her words. The pasta smelled and looked amazing. "Just some more drinks, please," Indira said as she gestured with her milk-coloured hand which was decorated with Wisteria-coloured nails, to the empty glasses.

"Same again?" The waitress asked, desperately trying to make eye contact with Indira.

"Yes," Indira said, finally granting the girl her wish, as her eyes fused with the woman's. The waitress's mouth parted ever so slightly and she blinked and looked away. "I'll get those for you right now," she sighed as though she had lost her breath.

Indira nodded and the waitress hurried off.

"Who?" I asked again, this time with a mouthful of pasta.

"The Burned Soul," she whispered.

I immediately felt Goosebumps engulf my body.

"That's why 'The Burned Soul' is trapped in a timeless part of the ends of the universe. He was too powerful to destroy. Possibly the most powerful being ever to exist other than God. The Time Aristocrats all worshiped him, but he is true evil," she explained.

"They all worshiped him?" I gasped.

"All except one," her voice saddened as she said it.

"Who?" I asked, but the waitress appeared between us as she placed the two cokes onto the table. This time she walked off without a glance or a word.

Indira looked down, folding her beautiful manicured hands together slowly on the table. Her mesmerising eyes flickered up at me from under her stunning dark-plum-coloured eyelashes.

I gulped down some more pasta with my folk.

"His name . . ." She paused, clearly reminiscing and feeling sad within her own mind . . . "Was, Jack Mayers."

I realized I was leaning towards her again unintentionally.

"You cared for this man?" I asked softly.

"Very much so," she murmured.

I reached forward instinctively and placed my hand onto her folded hands. She smiled at me briefly and then slipped her hands out from under mine, moving them away and under the table. I pulled my hand back, feeling a little embarrassed that I had touched her.

"Who is he?" I asked.

She smiled sadly, "the toughest and bravest man I had ever met."

"Where is he now?" I quizzed, not meaning to interrogate her.

"He's from a world that is very similar to this world, almost identical in fact. Except in that world magic doesn't really exist," Indira leant towards me, "Cornelius Strumple is not to be trusted!" She quickly warned.

"Who?" I asked, realising that she actually hadn't answered my question, but instead provided the perfect distraction with a warning to change the subject.

"The Burned Soul," she clarified. "As your powers develop, he *will* reach out to you. Resist the urge. Do you understand me Eleni?" Her face turned cold, expressionless. Her voice was almost a whisper.

I felt the weight of anxiety plummet onto me as my heart sank and my breathing paused. I quickly nodded.

"No matter what he offers you, resist the urge. Understood?"

I quickly nodded again.

"Cornelius Strumple is a deal maker, but every deal with that devil always has consequences," she cautioned.

I nodded for a third time as I gulped.

"I'm sorry if I frightened you child," Indira apologised warmly.

"I'm ok," I shrugged. "So am I a Stone Chaser and a 'Time Aristocrat?' then?"

Indira's eyes flickered and a shot of panic shot across her face. "Finish your pasta. It's time to go home now," she insisted.

"But . . ."

"Being able to wield two swords still needs investigation further by myself, the Reverend, and your father," she waved her hand and the waitress shot over like a bullet with the bill, smiling invitingly at her. Indira got out some cash and handed it, along with a generous tip, to the grateful waitress, who seemed to be in a bit of a muddle.

"Have a nice evening," she said lustfully.

"Thank you," Indira said without taking her eyes off of me. The waitress grimaced and walked away.

"Linx mentioned that only two people in history have ever been able to wield two different magic's," I piped up.

Indira frowned, "Did he say who?"

I nodded slowly.

"He shouldn't have burdened you with that Eleni. I'm sorry," her angel's face was grave.

"If 'Cornelius Strumple' is" . . .

"Don't say his name," her eyes were flared and panicked. "*I shouldn't have even said it.*"

Just then the door flung open and a cold wind flew in from outside. The host quickly shut it firmly. I found myself with a chill, and it wasn't from the wind.

"If you know who," I paused and gulped, "The burned soul," I whispered, "Is as powerful as God, then how is he trapped?"

"The entire universe ganged up on him and wiped out his small army of 'Time Aristocrats' and witches that worshiped him. Every wizard, sorcerer, angel, holy man and woman and warrior from every realm, used up almost every singe last ounce of magic left in the galaxy, to trap that monster in the furthest ends of time. Without his sword he can't manipulate the time-magic, but someone as powerful as him, will always have influences and manipulations somewhere. No doubt he'll sense your ability Eleni, and no doubt at some point he'll try and reach out through some vile supernatural means," she explained. "Enough about that fiend, even talking about him could bring evil down upon us. Eat up!" She commanded.

"How did you know where to find me and rescue me from those creeps?" I asked to change the subject as I swallowed down the last bit of pasta that was on my plate.

Indira grinned her gleaming white teeth and I wasn't sure how they looked so white in-between those Claret coloured lips and against that milky-skin. Her pigmentation was so pale that I would have expected her teeth to have an illusion of a tint of yellow to them, but they were pearly.

"I have been keeping tabs on you," she admitted.

I wondered if it should bother me that someone has been watching me and possibly stalking me, but due to who it was, I felt somewhat chuffed.

"Why?" I asked as I tried not to grin as we got up and walked out.

Indira sighed, almost as if she didn't want to say it, "Because you have more natural and raw magical ability inside of you, than I've ever seen in anyone else. You *and* Jade, but with Jade it is expected, given that she is the prophecy . . . But you Eleni, you are a mystery to us all."

And within a click of her fingers I was back inside the castle and alone in my bedroom. I still had her cardigan on and could smell her amazing scent. I felt all warm and fuzzy and tingly as I breathed in her gorgeous aroma. It brought a massive grin to my face. Suddenly without any sign of warning, the temperature dropped and it had gotten very cold all of a sudden. I found myself thinking of all the scary events that has happened since I came here and I just wished I was back in my boring simple life with Fiona on the farm. This place was awful and yet the people I have met so far have made me happy, sad, furious and aroused. I've made friends, enemies I think too, and as for Lingwood, Linx and certainly Indira – these were feelings I can't explain - odd feelings.

7- SMILING INTRUDER

An ominous jagged shape loomed like a demon of destruction in the black space just outside the porthole that led to earth. Inside this monstrous craft, Jealousaw sat alone in a tiny spherical room. A single streak of light gleamed on his hideous greyish-black helmet-like-mask as he sat motionless in his raised meditation chamber.

As General Mcgraft approached, the sphere opened bit by bit, as though Jealousaw knew he was there, despite having his back to the General. The upper half of the sphere lifted up slowly like a jagged-toothed mechanical jaw and the picture of a beautiful woman that was spread across a screen in front of Jealousaw, quickly vanished. The dark figure seated inside the mouth-like cocoon barely seemed alive as it sat stationary. There was no doubt in the General's mind that sat in front of him with its back to him, was pure evil. It emanated from him – the aura of sheer power and true wickedness radiated the room, sending a chilling fear through the officer.

"What is it General?!" A deep powerful voice flooded the room. The General straightened up and gulped, uncertain of his own courage - Mcgraft took a hesitant step forward. He had news to tell Jealousaw, but felt prepared to wait before delivering his message. He'd wait hours if necessary rather than disturb the dreaded Jealousaw's alone-time.

"My lord," the General replied, choosing each word with extreme caution. "King Kane of the Ice-Lords demands an audience," he already regretted using the word demand and shut his eyes briefly. Jealousaw stood, rising to his full three-metre height, his cloak swaying against the floor.

"As he wishes," the deep voice erupted, "Leave!" He ordered.

"Yes my lord," the General bowed a quick nod of the head and twisted sharply, power-walking out of the door.

Jealousaw activated a large screen.

"What is my bidding my King?"

"I want you to stop this madness Jealousaw. I know you feel the child has the potential power to help you locate 'The Burned Soul', but revenge won't bring back your wife!" The King barked.

"Cornelius Strumple has the power to resurrect," Furious, Jealousaw clenched his black-gloved-hands into fists. "It was my wife – *your* impractical daughter that proved that ability, when she scarified her life to do so. Remember?!" Jealousaw growled as regret flowed through him. "I owe your daughter and Cornelius my gratitude for this suffering monster I have become!"

"Invading Earth and kidnapping that small girl is dangerous. She has more potential power than even *you* Dark Lord," the King warned.

"Does she," he snarled enraged, "And you are certain, are you? That this child has more power than me?"

The King staggered back, his hand automatically reaching for his throat. A few seconds went past and The King began to gag as his throat, as if in the grip of invisible talons, began to constrict.

"Release him!" Queen Elana Kane demanded as she entered the picture.

"As you wish, my Queen," Jealousaw bowed with respect, the only person he truly took orders from was her - the mother that looked so much like her daughter Zoe, who he once loved so much.

"How dare you!" The King coughed as Jealousaw released him from his mind-choke.

"Oh shut up, you provoked him into it!" The Queen defended. The King looked up at her with despair and shock.

"Can she be turned to an ally? Then we wouldn't have to worry about the threat of her potential power?" The Queen suggested to Jealousaw.

"If her mind isn't already poisoned against me, then she could be an asset worthy of an apprentice – but I'll be the judge of that!" Jealousaw snarled.

"No," the King begged, "leave her be. If you don't attack then they'll have no reason to train her and she won't fulfil her potential! And . . . "

"Jealousaw will train her!" The Queen cut in.

"That's even worse!" The King groaned. "Even if you did succeed in turning her to our side, if you train her then there is a risk she'll become too powerful to control. Jealousaw, search your feelings, you know this to be true! Your presence near that girl is a danger to us all," the King pleaded.

"That child is the one chance we have of getting answers from 'The Burned Soul', possibly even our daughter back, and all you're worried about is her potential ability to overthrow us. She's a child for pity sake, she's no threat to us!" The Queen spat venomously.

"Children grow up!" The King warned.

"Don't be a coward!" She yelled.

"You needn't worry about her potential threat," Jealousaw's booming and powerful-heavy breathing voice bellowed. "I will use her to get the information we need by whatever means necessary. Either against her will, or by an alliance. The choice will be the child's. Then, after I have located 'This Burned Soul' I will kill them both!" Jealousaw hissed, and with that he switched off the screen, ending the chat. He twisted sharply and marched out of the room. "Captain Lanker. Where is General Mcgraft?" The Dark Lord demanded angrily.

"The shitter," the Captain said quickly without thinking.

"FIND ME THAT INTRUDER!!!!" He screamed with fury and the entire ship shook from the power that raged within him.

"Yes my lord," the captain gulped.

Lukamore had snuck out of the ventilation shaft and hid in the docking bay beneath the engine room. He felt the hate-magic radiate through the ship as the entire craft trembled.

And he smiled.

8- *FROZEN WITH TERROR*

It was extremely difficult, in the now-nearing morning, to dispute with the small part of me that was certain that last night didn't happen – that it was all a dream! Logic definitely wasn't on my side, or common sense. I clung to the sections of last night that I couldn't have imagined – like her incredible smell from her cardigan. I was adamant I could never have dreamed that up by myself.

It was misty and gloomy outside the window as usual in this godforsaken place, as light fought against the dimming darkness.

Indira had clicked her fingers and I was magically sprung back to my room – *alone* - to my disappointment. I sat, totally zombiefied as I glared at the wall for hours. It was now well into the early hours of the morning. Eventually, I snapped out of my daze, throwing myself onto my back on the springy and uncomfortable bed, once again zoning out, except this time I was gazing at the ceiling and not the wall. I had a silly smile from ear to ear like I had been dosed with some Joker-Toxin from the Batman comics.

"Are you ok?" A few female voices yelled through the door. They must have heard the squeak of the awful bed and the huge sigh that escaped as I sprung back onto it, spread out like a starfish.

"I'm fine," I said breathlessly.

"Can we come in?" They asked. – They must have been waiting up for me – I assumed.

"Sure!" I sighed, and with that, Sofia, Dotty, Estella, Stephanie and Jade, all poked their heads around the door. Their faces curious and dying to know what happened.

"She's so dreamy," I said pathetically with a huge grin.

"Who?" Sofia frowned, "Miss Amitola?"

"Yes," I breathed.

"You a lesbian?" Dotty asked with a hopeful expression on her face.

"I don't think so," I said before coming to my senses, "I mean, no!"

"I thought you liked Linx and Lingwood?" Jade piped up with a confused look.

"I do," I clarified, "but . . ."

"You swinging both ways?" Sofia cut in.

"She's just experimenting. We've all been there," Stephanie shrugged.

"No we haven't Steph!" Sofia corrected.

"Well there is nothing wrong with it," Dotty grumbled.

"Not at all," Sofia backpedalled.

"If Eleni wants to go *Vag*-etarian, then that leaves more meat for the rest of us," Stephanie sniggered.

We all rolled our eyes and giggled.

"So what happened then?" Estella finally spoke.

"We sat and had dinner," I replied.

"And now you're in love?" Sofia alleged sceptically.

"She has this odd aroma that makes you go weak at the knees. Don't tell me you didn't feel it when you saw her, because I know you all did," I argued. I was expecting some sort of resistance, but to my shock they all nodded and agreed.

"She's smoking hot stuff – *but*, I'd soooooo choose Linx all day long," Stephanie wheezed.

"What about Lingwood?" Sofia sniggered, "Or *any* man with a pulse!"

"Shut up!" Stephanie chuckled as she rolled her eyes.

"Have you texted Tom yet?" I asked, desperate to change the subject away from me.

"We are going to be late for school if we don't get showered and dressed soon," Sofia deflected. I looked at my watch and couldn't believe that we had been up all night.

"I bet she has!" Stephanie said playfully, waiting for Sofia to have another dig at how easy she is with the male population, - but to everyone's shock, Sofia smirked and blushed.

"OH MY GOD!!!" We all squealed with excitement.

"What did you say?" Jade asked eagerly.

"Did he reply?" Stephanie was ecstatic with anticipation.

"Have you both been texting each other?" Estella blurted with enthusiasm.

"Is he taking you to the dance?" I jumped in with equal thrill.

"No, I'm going to the dance alone!" She sighed, "And I just said *'hey, whatsup?'*" Sofia ended our exhilaration.

"Is that it?" Stephanie sounded really disappointed.

"Sorry that I didn't send him a nude, Stephanie! Not everyone is so desperate to get under the sheets!" Sofia moaned.

"With *your* body, you'd blow his mind," I complimented, but quickly shut up when Sofia frowned at me.

"Did he text back?" Jade intervened.

Sofia nodded and couldn't hide the smirk that was reappearing on her face.

"Well?" Stephanie asked impatiently.

Sofia sighed. "He texted me back *'hello stranger, I'm all good, how's you?*"

Stephanie rolled her eyes, "have you replied yet?"

Sofia shook her head.

"Good. Let him sweat a little," Stephanie advised.

"No, that's mean!" Jade protested.

"How is it mean? You might be busy. If he can't wait a few hours or go a day without hearing from you, then that's a red flag," Stephanie warned.

"I agree," Sofia said as she got up and walked out of the room. "Come on, we need to start getting ready for school."

I immediately yawned.

"Eleni can go last in the shower when there is no hot water left, as she needs to cool off from Miss Amitola," Stephanie joked.

The girls all giggled and got up and slowly left. I obeyed and waited until last to go into the shower, still laying on the bed in disbelief at my confused feelings.

I slowly walked out of the room, a heavy stupor still clouding my mind. I went through the motions of getting ready for school without paying any attention to what I was doing. It wasn't until I was in the shower - the arctic-water spraying my skin, freezing me – that I realised I was still in a trance. The frosty drench snapped me out of my daze with a devastating breathless iciness, causing me to gasp for air at the shock of the sudden cold. I shuddered violently for several minutes as I refused to give-in to my instincts of darting out from under this arctic-spray. My muscles were rigid and my skin pimpled from the bitterness as I washed. Finally after several minutes of suffering the coldness begun to feel refreshing, after what seemed like an eternity - and I let it soak into my eyes and hair. I eventually switched the freeze off and stumbled out of the shower, wrapping myself securely in a towel as I desperately tried to warn off the aching shivers, glistening what little warmth I could muster from the now-damp-towel. My mind still swirled and I felt lightheaded. I perched myself on the side of the bathtub as I hugged my arms for warmth. My brain was racked full of images of Linx, Lingwood, and now Indira. Suddenly Harry's beaming smile shot across my vision. I smiled instantly at the thought of his warm and happy grin, but quickly frowned and banished the young pup from my memory bank. Nothing seemed clear and I was so confused and distracted.

I rushed into my bedroom, teeth chattering, and quickly got dressed. I made sure I was completely dry before rapidly putting on as many layers that I could, to try and get rid of this freeze that had engulfed my body. I felt like *'The Michelin Man'* wrapped in all the heavy clothing, as it gave the impression that my entire body was made of tyre upon tyre due to the thick layers, but at this point I didn't care. – Then my girlie instincts kicked in as I looked in the mirror. – *I've made myself look mahoosive!* – I fretted. So I sat on the bed and waited until some warmth clung to me before removing a few layers. I might not be as snug, but at least I didn't look like *'Nellie The Elephant'* anymore. I was still colourless and ugly, but at least I wasn't colourless FAT and ugly. – Which is something, I suppose.

I finished off in the bathroom, brushing my teeth and sweeping the hairbrush painfully through my knotted and damp hair. I had no time to dry it properly this morning as I was already running late. I flung it back in a tight ponytail and sighed with frustration. – *I wish I was prettier!*

When I got downstairs nobody was around. I was later than I had realized and knew that at any minute my wrist was going to start that aching pulse from one of the tormenting teachers. I rapidly grabbed a Health Bar from my rucksack and munched it down, almost swallowing it whole – *Stephanie would be proud* – I giggled inside my head as I gulped it in three hasty bites. – No time for a drink - so I hung my head under the tap and let a few splashes clench my morning thirst, then rushed off to school. Hopefully the inevitable storm that was coming would hold off until I located the girls. It was unusually misty; the fog was almost like thick white smoke. The steamy haze was ice cold as it clung to the exposed skin of my face and neck. Now I wished I had dried my hair better as it felt as though my head was going to form into a solid block of ice. The thick freezing vapour stung my eyes. I found myself placing my hands out in front of me as though I were blind. I couldn't see a thing as the white mist swooped around me. I found shivers trickling down my spine as my body went arctic with fear as I thought about that horror movie *'The Fog'*.

Suddenly I had a lump in my throat and despite the freezing mist, I was sweating and panting as terror gripped my body in a vice.

Suddenly without warning he was there, walking along side me.

"Do you mind if I walk with you?" He asked, amused by my expression of surprise and uncertainly as he startled me.

"Lingwood," I gasped as I held my hand to my heart. "You scared the shit out of me!"

"Sorry," he apologised but his smug smirk remained intact.

All of a sudden my heart fluttered. His simple, loose, royal blue t-shirt moulded to his muscular chest and arms perfectly and his blue jeans hugged his body in all the ways they should on a man. I found myself seriously turned on and this petrified me – *My hormones are all over the place! What is wrong with me?* Then I gasped out loud and he frowned at me with confusion – *shit he can read minds! He probably knows what I just thought!!!* – I panicked.

"I want to ask you something!" I said firmly, "Just one question." I needed to distract my curious mind that was wondering to all the wrong places this morning.

"Go ahead," he urged as the smug expression vanished from his chops. Clearly my abruptness caught him off-guard.

"You and your father can read minds, right?" It felt like such a stupid question but I had a point that I was getting to.

"To a degree, yes," he admitted, "Was that the question?"

"No! – Well, yes . . ." I stalled, "How does it work?"

He looked at me with disapproval. "What do you mean?"

"Well, exactly that. If you read minds then why do you need to ask me what I mean?" I made my point smugly.

"I think you'll find that's more than one question," he pointed out with a smirk.

I frowned and remained silent, waiting for his reply.

I can't read everybody's mind from all over the place. I have to be close by to them," he clarified.

I gulped.

"What's it like?" I pleaded for information.

"It's like loads of people talking at once. I can only read minds when I focus on an individual," he replied.

"Is there anyone's mind that you can't read?" I asked.

"Only those that have the immense power to block it, but rarely have I met anyone with *that* sort of ability. It takes a lot out of you to block a mind-read," he explained.

"Ok, what am I thinking?" I asked with a grin.

He frowned hard. He looked right at me and my heart skipped a beat. His eyes were enigmatic and mine were wide open with fright at how I had butterflies in my stomach. What was wrong with me?

"For some reason your mind is difficult to read. I can sense your thoughts were very terrified last night followed by," he paused.

"By what?" I asked.

"By lust," he sounded confused.

"Lust," I giggled.

"Yes," he confirmed, his face then tightened, "And now you are conflicted with your feelings. It's my turn for some questions."

I swallowed hard – but when I looked at him his honey-eyes were soft and gentle, but he looked sad. – *Fuck, his eyes were intense!* – I suddenly lost my chain of thought as he spoke, I didn't hear.

"W-wha?" Were the only words I could muster as I got lost in his eyes.

"I said, who were you with last night?" He chuckled.

"Myself and the girls went to the beach, I met Harry and he reckons you're a vampire," I snickered nervously, "And then I went shopping with the girls and out to eat with Indira."

He grinned, clearly amused. "Harry thinks I'm a Vampire?"

"Yes," I chuckled nervously again.

"Well, maybe I am," he smiled ruefully at me. His velvety voice was compelling.

My heart stopped for just a second.

"So, why are your feelings so conflicted?" He asked.

I tried not to look at his handsome face as his intense eyes were making my bones turn soft.

"I dunno," I shrugged.

"Indira," he mumbled. "I get it," he nodded. "She *is* beautiful." His face looked as though he was in pain and trying to hide it.

"What am I thinking now though?" I seductively said in a pathetic attempt at flirting to try to get through to his thick skull that I actually like him just as much, if not more. He was right about one thing, my feelings *were* very conflicted. I needed to compose myself here. He seemed to radiate sexiness this morning and it was making my heart go flip-flop and you wouldn't have to be a mind reader to see it. – *Stupid traitorous heart!* – I frowned.

"You should listen to Harry and stay well clear of me," he suddenly warned, and with that he had disappeared inside the mist. He was gone! Now I felt really confused. I was caught somewhere between sadness that I'd clearly upset him and disappointment that he'd gone, but the one thing that stood out the most, was why should I listen to Harry? I gulped as suddenly realisation hit me at what I told Lingwood about what Harry had said. I'd only mentioned one word –

'Vampire!'

I went to class and got there in the nick-of-time. I spent the entire class distracted and learning nothing. Was Lingwood a Vampire? Was his warning genuine? Is he good? Or is he bad? The rest of that morning went in a bit of a blur. I had a class with Jade and Estella but can barely remember it.

It was lunch time now and I had spent the entire morning completely and utterly distracted. My mind kept wondering to Inidra the night before and now also Lingwood. I found tears escaping my eyes as I felt really fed up. I have never had a relationship – boy or girl! It's always just been me, mum and Fiona . . . and now here I was, unhealthily fixated on two - possibly three people!

I spotted Sofia in the library getting some books and went to walk over, but I stopped instantly as I spotted Tom lurking. I observed with a smirk as she clearly tried to avoid him. I could suddenly sense her embarrassment as she went to buy the books and didn't have enough cash.

"Oh, can I leave these here and run back to get more money?" She flustered. I could hear from the croak in her voice that her throat was dry as I spotted tears burning her eyes. I went to walk over and help, but then I saw his towering presence. I could see from the look on Sofia's face that she wished to become invisible. Tom's height towered over her.

"Is there a problem?" His deep voice asked, and although Sofia was the toughest girl I know, I recognised that look as her heart clearly skipped a beat. It was the same look I had every time Lingwood, Lynx or Indira were near me. Her eyes fluttered and she held her breath as he spoke, clearly there wasn't something wrong with me that I found voices of those I liked alluring. Clearly Sofia was finding his masculine voice very alluring, despite doing her best to hide all emotion. I knew the look, I knew it well.

"Yeah, there is a problem, she doesn't have enough," the cashier groaned. *Big mistake mate* – I thought with a chuckle. Sofia's glare could have burned the room.

"No! I told you there is no problem, idiot! I just need to put these to one side and go get a little extra cash from my dorm!" She snapped. Her anger hid it well, but I could see through her barriers now and could sense her humiliation. Her glare had told the cashier all he needed to know, *which was shut up.* His face dropped and if I didn't know better I'd had guessed he had shit his pants.

Tom placed his books down beside Sofia.

"Why are you here?" She groaned with despair.

"Errr, to buy books, obviously," he replied sarcastically with a chuckle. "Here, ring mine up too," he pulled out a Santander card and set it on the counter. "I'll get both of ours."

"What! Did you think I needed a handout?" Sofia barked, "Thanks, but no. I have enough back in my room."

"It's freezing and misty out there, I'll save you the trouble." he suggested.

"What are you, my mother?" Sofia snapped. I could see the cringe in her eyes, she knew she was being rude and clearly didn't mean it. But I could almost spot the clogs turning inside her head. She didn't understand why he was being so nice and was clearly panicked by what he'd want in return.

"I won't sleep with you!" She blurted.

The cashier snorted and covered it with a cough.

"Holy-shit," a few of his mates sniggered from nearby.

"Who said I wanted to sleep with you?" He replied with a smirk as he flung his rucksack over his shoulder. I couldn't help but grin, Tom handled Sofia so perfectly. Most guys, people - in fact, can't handle her moodiness and confrontation, but here was a guy that found it all so amusing. This clearly unsettled her and she can hide it all she likes, but I could see that this attracted her to him.

Did I just see Sofia gulp? The fearless Sofia, almost dumbstruck. This was amusing me more than it should.

"Or blow jobs!" She mumbled. "Anything sexual is off the table." I could see by the way she clenched her eyes shut for a

brief second that she wanted to shut up. The horror written
across her own face at her own words was almost hilarious. It
was like looking in a mirror at how I behaved around
Lingwood and Lynx. Oh and Indira. I gritted my teeth as I
quickly banished them from my thoughts to continue to watch.
She clearly really liked him as all logic seemed to have
vanished from this usual very logical and outspoken girl.
Tom's friends tried not to laugh, but the smirks slid across
their faces anyway. Tom tried to hide his own blush as his face
turned a little red. He quickly slid the card towards the
stunned cashier and rapidly paid, before turning to her,
holding out his hand. Sofia glared down at his hand.

"I'm not shaking your hand," she snorted – at that moment he
quickly grabbed her hand - to her horror, and kissed it. I
thought she was going to slap him but I saw the electric buzz
shoot through her when their skin touched.

"I held my hand out because I was going to carry your bag for
you," he chuckled as he shook his head, "But as you've been so
nice, I thought I'd kiss your hand instead," he joked.

"You don't think I can handle it?" She asserted. I couldn't tell if
Sofia was winding him up or not, or if she was serious.

"What? No," he backpedalled. "That's not what I meant."

"I've lifted weights six times heavier than these stupid books!"
Sofia grumbled.

"I can tell. You look great," he deflected her mood once again
perfectly with a playful smirk. *God he's good!* – I thought as I

continued to watch how impressively he handled Sofia. I don't think she knew what to do. I'm certain she's never had anyone handle her so perfectly. She tried to hide her blush at the compliment but I could see she was delighted that he had noticed her body.

"So what did you mean?" She tried to maintain her anger.

"Well . . ." He paused . . . "You're a."

"A what?" She cut in.

"A lady."

My heart melted when he said that, and I think secretly so did Sofia's.

"I'm a *lady*. *Who* uses the word *lady*. I'm a woman!" She scorned.

"You certainly are," he deflected her anger once more with a playful flirty smirk as he regarded her lustfully. I'm not sure what angered her more – the fact that she couldn't stay angry due to him taking nothing she said seriously - or at herself for what she had said earlier about the sexual acts.

"So, because I'm a *lady* I need a strong, burly man like you to help me. Is that what you're saying?" Sofia had his balls in a vice now. "Do you consider me helpless?" I couldn't tell if Sofia was infuriated or just tugging his leg. Sofia was cruel enough to be doing either.

Tom finally went bright red as he blew out a long sigh of breath.

"I was trying to be a gentleman to you."

Sofia tried to hide her smirk, but I saw the corners of her mouth tilt upwards ever so slightly. "I can pay you back," she said with annoyance, to clearly change tact before she blushed. "Well, you can pay me back by allowing me to take you out for lunch," Tom insisted, "Perhaps dinner?" Even though they couldn't see me I nodded my approval at Tom's persistence and the way he coolly extinguished Sofia's hot-headed flame. "Can't do lunch right now, I have no money," Sofia smiled smugly.

"And dinner?" Tom was smoother than James Bond.

For the first time ever, I spotted complete lust in Sofia's eyes as she eyed him curiously, "I'm busy in the evenings," – *Oh she was making him work for it!*

"Well, you have my number if you change your mind," he handled the rejection perfectly as he grabbed his rucksack and walked off with his mates, acting as though he didn't care, a master class on how to handle difficult women.

Sofia snatched the books off of the shelf and hurried off, tears were in her eyes.

"Well that was smooth," I giggled as I approached her.

"Shut up and go away!" She said, but her voice lacked its usual threatening conviction. I ignored her and hugged her tight.

"I'm fine!" She insisted, but I heard the choke in her voice.

"You really like him, don't you?" I stated.

Sofia shrugged, "I've still not quite forgiven him for dunking me," she chuckled sadly.

I laughed, "I think you got your revenge when you tugged his shorts down," I reminded her.

We both giggled and I had succeeded in cheering her up.

"So are you going to take him up on his offer?" I dug.

"What, and end up getting used and abused or my heart destroyed. Why would I want to do that? I'm perfectly happy on my own," she declared.

"Who hurt you?" I asked boldly.

"Nobody. This is just how I am. And it's none of *your* business anyway!" She put me back in my place.

"Jeeeeez! Sorry!!!" I snapped.

"Just leave me alone Eleni. OK! Focus on your own love triangle or whatever fucked up shit is going on with you," Sofia was angry but a sob had built up as she yelled. I was done trying to hug her and make things better by this stage.

"FINE!" I growled as I marched off in a strop.

I stormed into the canteen raging. Tom was sitting at a table with his mates and spotted me.

"Hey Eleni?" He called out.

I sighed, "What?"

"Ouch, bad day?" He asked as he got up and offered me a seat.

"I'm fine thanks, and I don't need a seat," I pushed the chair back under the table.

"Ok, may I walk with you a moment then?" He asked. His mates smirked and sniggered to each other.

"Shut up," he chuckled back at them. "May I walk with you?" He asked again.

"It's a free country," I shrugged grumpily. Oh god I was beginning to sound like Sofia.

"It is," he chuckled. "So, what's the deal with your friend?"

"Sofia?" I snorted angrily, "Good luck with *that one,* pal!" I groaned and then immediately regretted it. "She likes you," I reassured him, backpedalling from my rage at her. "You just have to be patient with her."

I hoped I wasn't giving him false optimism.

"Ok," he nodded. "Thank you."

"You're welcome," I smiled sweetly and he turned and walked back to join his mates.

His coolness and calmness was so perfect for Sofia, perhaps that was what scared her so much. I now felt a little bad at stomping off like I had done. Sofia was clearly finding this hard and I knew better than to take her moodiness personally. Especially when she told me about being a mind-fairy. This meant she often feels everybody's feelings constantly, good or bad. No wonder she's always stressed. I can't imagine the burden of feeling everybody's pain as though it were your own. She was the strongest character I knew just to get up in the mornings.

Suddenly to my horror Vladimir appeared alongside me. His dark caped-coat was like Dracula as it swooped around him. "Tell me everything," he commanded.

"What do you mean?" I asked, gobsmacked.

"What happened this morning?"

"With what?" I played dumb as I had a slight incline of what he was getting at.

"My son!" His teeth gritted as he said it.

"What about your son?" I replied sternly.

He glared at me, his expression stiff with scepticism. "You like him?"

"Yes," I said curtly.

His lips puckered in disappointment. "Really like him?" He probed.

"Yes," I said again, blushing.

"And he seems very fond of you," he pointed out.

"Really?" I said eagerly, making myself sound completely and ridiculously desperate.

"And you aren't afraid of him?" Vladimir seemed suspiciously curious as he looked right at me.

"You can read my mind, you tell me!" I growled, still a little fired up from my confrontation with Sofia.

"You know what we are?" He whispered, his voice sounding intimidating and scary.

I gulped, "What are you?" But I knew that he could read my thoughts and what I was thinking right now – *Vampire!*

He smiled, "Lingwood doesn't usually play with his food," and with that he walked off leaving me frozen with terror.

9- RETURNING THE KISS

Father, Indira, all the teachers and even Reverend Crone were watching from the sidelines as Linx trained us all with swords, our particle-manipulator teacher Jenifer Hoax, also trained us with magic, before the tournament would begin.

"I know we have worked you hard lately, but we need to prepare you for the horrors that are coming. You students have come on in leaps and bounds and we are all very proud of you," Miss Hoax stated as she stepped forward - her black cloak blowing in the wind alongside her long white hair.

"The tournament is about to start. Prepare yourselves as I announce who will go up against whom. I will personally be refereeing these fights and I will allow any means necessary to defeat your opponent. However, when I say the bout is over, then it is over. I don't want any unnecessary injuries. Do I make myself clear?" Linx spoke.

God he looked handsome in his tight black vest and black shorts. His muscles bulged as he held out his sword.

"I have placed a spell over all of you that will last just for this tournament. It means that you can't die during this tournament. However . . . you will still feel all the pain of injuries. So don't be reckless just because you can't be killed, the pain you will feel won't be worth it!" Miss Hoax warned.

"Basically, if you receive a blow that would usually kill you, you'll wish it did!" Linx chuckled, "Sofia, you're up first and you will fight Charlie."

Everybody shuffled into a good seated position to get a good and clear view of the arena.

Sofia stood up confidently and walked to the centre of the ring as Charlie slowly got to his feet a little unsteady.

"Take your sword," Linx nodded to him.

Charlie nodded and grabbed his sword, stepping into the arena.

Both their Ice-blades glistened brightly.

"BEGIN!" Linx bellowed.

Sofia made the first move, instantly lashing out with an angry swipe towards Charlie. The ginger-haired boys face was riddled with panic as he just got out of the way.

"Remember your training Charlie!" Reverend Crone yelled from the crowd.

Sofia lashed out again with a swinging wallop! This time Charlie lifted his sword to meet hers. Sparks flew as the ice-swords clashed and Charlie cunningly flung out a leg, kicking Sofia in the stomach and then punching her to the floor. Sofia leapt up and with utter rage slammed her fist into the ground. An energy-wave of ice shot out of her and towards Charlie, lifting the boy off of his feet and sending him plummeting to the ground. She leapt towards him furiously, but Charlie rolled out of the way as her Ice sword planted itself into the earth.

Charlie swept his foot round in an attempt to trip her legs from under her, but Sofia's reflexes were good and she jumped over his sweeping leg, tugging her sword free from the floor. She swung her sword wildly and angrily at him again. He frantically tried to block it but his sword flung from his grip. Charlie crawled backwards away from her in desperate panic. "Yield!" Sofia demanded as she held the point of her sword to his throat. Charlie nodded quickly.

"Coward!" Reverend Crone shouted from the crowd.

"Sofia is the winner," Linx announced, "Next up is Stacy and Peter."

Wolf-whistles were heard coming from the crowd as Stacy strutted up to the arena. Her incredible figure stood there with the sun setting behind her as she studied her painted nails.

"No high-heels in the arena!" Linx barked.

"Oh please. If I take these off your foot-fetish will distract you Linx," Stacy giggled as she refused to remove her heels.

Linx just shook his head at her and she blew him a seductive kiss. Oh how I really hated her!

Peter rushed up to the ring, his eyes bulging at her good-looks.

"Begin!" Linx announced.

Peter grinned as he stepped towards the beauty. His stone-sword held tightly in his grip. Stacy hadn't even taken her sword out and I wondered what she was. Ice-lord most likely with *her* frosty personality – I assumed.

"Hey handsome," Stacy flirted as she fluttered her long black eyelashes at him, "You're not going to hurt me, are you?"

"Get your sword out!" Peter hesitated.

Suddenly Stacy blew him a kiss and clicked her fingers. Peter fell to the floor in agony clutching his groin. Everybody winced as Stacy closed her palm.

"I yield!" Peter screamed in agony.

"Stacy is the winner," Linx announced and she smugly went and sat back down and begun painting her fingernails.

"Next up is Dotty and Sally!"

The black haired woman frowned angrily and Dotty gulped.

"COME ON DOTTY!!!!" We all yelled, showing our encouragement.

"Begin!" Linx commanded.

Sally brushed her long black hair out of her eyes and smiled evilly.

Dotty's hand trembled slightly as she gripped her stone-sword. Sally flung her ice-sword towards Dotty and Dotty shut her eyes with fright. She swung her stone-blade around and around as she spun on her heels, as though she were going to throw it. Dotty eventually went dizzy and tumbled to the ground – when she finally opened her eyes, Sally was unconscious on the floor.

"Well done," Linx chuckled as he helped the bewildered Dotty off of the soil. "Next time don't shut your eyes and hold your breath," he chuckled.

Dotty puffed out her cheeks as she went and threw up.

"Next up is Harold and our reigning champion, Lingwood," Linx announced.

I sat up a little straighter as I watched Lingwood coolly walk into the arena. It didn't take long for Lingwood to defeat Harold skilfully and swiftly without even breaking a sweat, reminding everybody why he was the champ. I couldn't help but feel even more attraction towards him after watching how strong and quick he was. He hadn't even taken his sword out and I wondered what he was.

Next up was Stephanie versus Eric. The flaming redhead's fire was too much for the Stone-chaser to handle and he was soon defeated. Eric brushed his long blonde hair to the side and embarrassingly rushed out of the arena.

Estella was next and she fought Lisa. It was a close fight, but Estella just edged it and won when she used her wooden sword to wield plant magic to trap Lisa into submission. The redheaded Ice-lord didn't stand a chance once she had dropped her sword.

Next up was Jade and Jim. I could see the nervousness in Jade's bright blue eyes as her long blonde hair twirled around her in the wind. Her pink and white Unicorn sword glowed brightly as Jim stepped towards her. He gripped his Stone-sword tightly as he smashed it into the earth, the vibrations causing Jade to lose her footing and tumble to the ground. She desperately tried to reach her sword that had slipped from her grasp as Jim swung aggressively towards her. Jim was a big lad, his belly bigger than Jade's entire body, which made him slow, but powerful. Jade rolled out of the way of his hammer-motion as his stone-sword imbedded itself into the soil with a dent. She picked up her bright pink and white sword and there was a huge flashing pink light. Everyone squinted and closed their eyes from the sizzling pink glow and when the light stopped, Jim was flat out on the floor.

"Well done!" Linx complimented Jade.

"Next is Eleni . . ." Linx paused for a split second and I could see the frustration written on his face, ". . . Versus our reigning champion, Lingwood."

My heart froze. I went cold all over and suddenly felt sick. He smugly walked out into the arena and waited for me. I staggered to my feet and unstably stumbled over my own legs until I got to the arena. The nerves made me incredibly unsettled, especially as his gorgeous grin smirked my way. I tried to conceal my blush and not look at his honey-coloured eyes.

"Make this quick Lingwood, and don't you dare hurt her!" Linx whispered.

"Down boy," Lingwood whispered back to an enraged Linx.

"Begin!" Linx growled.

Lingwood didn't make a move towards me and placed his wooden sword onto the ground.

"I yield," he said as he walked out of the arena. *He was a Wood-Fairy like Estella!*

Everyone was speechless as Lingwood disappeared from sight as he walked through the booing crowd.

"The champion is out!!!" Linx then yelled, trying to hide the delight in his voice. "Next up is Sofia and Tom!"

I spotted the excitement in Tom's eyes and the nervousness on Sofia's, as they both stepped into the ring.

"You look excited by me," Tom joked.

Sofia became infuriated.

"Sorry to disappoint!" She said, her cheeks now reddened in anger, "You certainly don't excite me! That's why I still haven't texted you."

"Well, *you* certainly excite me!" He smirked, "And it was *you* that initiated the texting. All I did was hand you my number with the hope to hear from you and see your pretty face again. I'd be very disappointed if you hadn't had texted me, but I told you to only message me if you're interested. If you're not interested, then I'm sorry to hear that. Like I say, you've got my number if you change your mind," he shrugged as though he didn't care and I saw Sofia's face drop.

"Oh, please. Save your flattery for someone who cares!" Sofia retaliated, hiding her blush well. "I won't change my mind!"

"Well, what did you expect when you texted me?" Tom grinned, "I'm hardly going to be horrible to you, and I certainly don't want to be *just* your texting buddy. Or is that what you expect from guys?"

"I texted you one time, get over it. I don't expect anything," Sofia said indignantly, "Except to be left alone!"

"Well, for someone that wants to be left alone, you're standing rather close," he pointed out.

Embarrassed to realise that she was indeed, standing rather close to him, she gently backed away, but not in a hurry, which gave Tom the impression, as well as me, that she wasn't *too* uncomfortable at being in his personal space.

The crowd grew restless.

"Hey! Are we fighting here, or having a domestic?" Linx whispered to them.

"Look, Sofia, I think you are great. So I'm going to do a deal with you so that you can get what you want, ok?" Tom suggested, ignoring Linx and the crowd.

She stood with her arms folded, her face a little flushed, "And what is it I want?"

"Only you can know *that*, princess," he said charmingly.

"Fine!" She grunted.

"The deal is . . . If I beat you I get to take you out on that date," he teased as he poked his tongue out at her playfully.

"You won't win!" She growled angrily, but she couldn't help herself but ask, "And what if I beat you?"

"If you beat me, then I get to give you a kiss and if you don't like it, then you can return it," he winked at her, "Deal?"

Sofia's grumpy face couldn't stop her surprise smirk that she just couldn't contain any longer.

"But what happens if I like it?" She instinctively flirted, then frowned at her own words in disbelief that she had said them.

"BEGIN!!!" Linx yelled, finally having enough, "Or both forfeit!"

Tom slowly stepped towards Sofia as he held up his Stone-Chaser sword.

"If you like it, then I'll give you more kisses, but first you have to beat me," he said cockily as he blew her a kiss. "You can have that one for free."

Sofia tried not to grin and blush, irritated that this relentless guy was slowly breaking down her barriers and seemed unaffected by anything she threw at him.

"I might forfeit now then. I'd rather sit and eat a meal with you than have *you* kiss me. I don't like *you!* Get that through your thick skull!"

"But what if I forfeit first? You'll have to honour our deal," Tom said playfully, unfazed once again by her stinging words.

"I don't have to honour anything. We never shook on it!" Sofia grinned smugly.

"Can we have some fighting please!!!" Linx yelled, "Final warning!"

"Ladies first," Tom insisted as he bowed his head.

Sofia leapt towards Tom with her Ice-blade glistening brightly. Tom blocked it with ease.

"You're holding back," he teased.

"So are you!" She replied as their swords locked together.

"God you are beautiful," he said to her as he gazed into her hazel eyes.

I spotted Sofia gulp. I could see that Sofia felt suddenly unexpectedly shy. Her cheeks flushed pink and, when she realised she was blushing, she averted her eyes. Whether Tom meant that as a distraction or not, I wasn't sure - but nonetheless, Sofia *was* distracted. Tom quickly overpowered her as he pushed her sword back towards her. Sofia rapidly snapped out of her momentary trance and aggressively and furiously swiped her Ice-Blade, knocking Tom's sword from his grip. Tom held out both hands by his side as he took measured steps away from her. Sofia held the tip of her blade to his throat.

"Yield," she demanded with a smug smile.

Tom then unexpectedly grabbed the end of her sword with his hands, the crowd gasped – as his palms burnt and split from the coldness of the Ice-Blade as he pushed her sword to the side. Not caring about the splitting Ice-burn to his hands, he leant in, merging his lips with hers in a passionate unsuspecting kiss. Sofia almost dropped her sword as her bones nearly turned to jelly. He slowly pulled his lips away from hers, "I yield," he whispered as he backed away and dropped to his knees.

Sofia was almost speechless. "How dare you!" She wheezed, horrified that he had stolen a kiss from her.

Tom winked at her cheekily and Sofia then glanced towards his frozen hands and her lips parted in a gasp. She then frowned back up at him for his stupidity.

"Sofia is the winner!" Linx announced as Miss Hoax stepped into the arena to heal Tom's hands with her magic. She led him away to a tent on the other side of the arena. Sofia stood motionless as she watched him.

"Next is Dotty versus Stacy," Linx announced.

We all gulped as Dotty nervously stepped into the ring. Her hand shook with fear as she gripped her heavy stone sword. Stacy strutted in confidently and yawned.

"Begin!" Linx commanded.

Stacy was still looking towards her nails as Dotty slowly stepped towards her.

"Why don't you just surrender now spotty," Stacy sniggered.

"My name is Dotty!!!" She yelled angrily as she swiped her stone-blade towards Stacy. The stunning blond clicked her fingers and vanished. The crowd gasped as Stacy reappeared behind Dotty and with one brisk movement grabbed Dotty's head, snapping her neck.

"NOOOOOOOOOO!!!!!!!!" Sofia screamed with fury as several people held her back. Stephanie, Jade, Estella and I, all sobbed. Even though we knew she couldn't actually die due to the spell that Miss Hoax had cast - watching Dotty's neck break was still heart wrenching and awful.

"Next up, we have Eleni versus Estella," Linx called out.

I would love to say that I was still distracted by the horror of watching my friend's neck snap, but if truth be said, Estella outwitted me. As soon as Linx had shouted "BEGIN", Estella had used her Earth-Magic to rise plants up from the ground. They instantly wrapped around my feet, ankles, legs and arms, trapping me. Just like a Python squeezing someone to death, the plants hugged me tighter and tighter until I dropped my sword. Estella then slowly walked up to me and held her wooden sword to my throat.

"Yield," she demanded, and the fight was over.

"I think that's a new record of fastest ever defeat," Linx sniggered to me. I frowned up at him but couldn't help a smirk at his charming boyish looks. My smirk soon faded as I spotted fathers face, disappointment was written all over his features as he shook his head at me.

"Next is Stephanie versus Sofia," Linx announced.

Sofia leapt into the ring and Stephanie strutted in, her long red hair blew impressively behind her as her Fire-blade lit up.

"Fire versus Ice. This should be interesting," Linx spoke, hyping up the crowd.

I saw father whispering to Indira and her nodding. I couldn't work out what they were talking about, but Reverend Crone ploughed through the crowd toward me.

"Reverend," I said respectfully with a nod as he stood next to me.

"You could have defeated that plant magic, Eleni. You, Stephanie, Jade and Sofia have the most potential I have seen since before even your father's time. If only we had more time before Jealousaw got here, we'd stand a chance with you girls. Sadly you're nowhere near ready," he grumbled.

"What about Estella and Dotty?" I asked.

"What about them?" He groaned.

"Do they not have potential too?"

"Yes, yes. Estella is very powerful and Dotty is very strong, but they're nothing special. Stephanie is the first Flame-Lord in over a decade. Fire-magic was thought to be almost extinct thanks to Jealousaw. She offers hope. Sofia's undeniable rage makes her strong. Jade's the chosen one with the rarest ability known to anyone . . . and, you . . ." He paused when he looked at me, unsure what to say.

"Yes, I know. Indira already told me that I am a conundrum," I mumbled.

"Indeed you are child. Indeed you are. Come to the main hall tonight at 7.30pm. I'll see to it that the guards let you in," he instructed.

I nodded and he rapidly pushed his way back through the crowd.

"Begin!" Linx ordered.

Stephanie immediately took Sofia by surprise as she flung fire towards her. Sofia leapt out of the way just in time and then sprinted angrily towards the redhead.

Stephanie ducked under Sofia's swinging strike and once again used fire-power to propel her. Sofia just barely blocked the fire with her Ice-Blade.

"Are you going to actually engage in a sword fight here? Or are you going to just keep spraying fire at me?" Sofia growled.

"I don't care for playing with swords much. I might break a nail," Stephanie grinned.

"You've played with plenty of swords in your time," Sofia mocked.

"I've kinda had enough of you calling me a slut," Stephanie growled as she struck her sword angrily towards Sofia without thinking.

The bald headed Latino ducked under her strike and stabbed her through the stomach with her Ice-blade.

"You shouldn't have let me bait you like that Steph. I couldn't get near you with your fire spray and you would have gotten me eventually, but I knew you sucked at sword-fighting and if I could get you emotionally involved enough to attack me, then that was the only chance I had to defeat you. And you fell for it hook line and sinker," Sofia said as she tugged her blade free from Stephanie who dropped to the floor.

"Well done Sofia. Not just a pretty face with a bad temper. You showed great intelligence there to gain the upper hand," Linx complimented. Sofia smirked as she walked off, I could see she was chuffed that Linx had called her pretty.

"Next is Estella versus Stacy!" Linx called out.

"Go get her!" Sofia snarled to Estella.

"Do this for Dotty!" I encouraged.

Estella nodded and stepped into the ring.

Stacy's perfect curves wiggled gracefully as she strutted up to the arena.

"Begin!" Linx yelled.

Estella instantly did the same trick she had done on me as plants rose from the ground, trapping Stacy. The gorgeous blond didn't struggle like I did. Instead she stood motionless as Estella walked up to her, holding her wooden sword to her throat, "Yield!"

Stacy puckered her lips and blew out a kiss. Suddenly Estella flew back through the air, landing with a thud on her back. The plants rapidly released Stacy from their clutch and she strutted slowly towards Estella who was climbing to her feet.

Estella went to grab her wooden sword that had slipped from her grasp, but Stacy with just the power of her mind, pierced Estella right through the heart with her own wooden sword.

We all stood gobsmacked on the sidelines as Stacy giggled.

"Next is Jade versus Sofia!" Linx called out, "The winner will face Stacy in the final!"

"I want Stacy! I will not hold anything back!!!" Sofia snarled to Jade.

"You've never liked me anyway!" Jade growled.

"Begin!" Linx bellowed.

Sofia darted towards Jade, slicing her Ice-Blade through the air. Jade held up her pink and white unicorn powered sword and there was an explosion as the Ice-blade connected with it. Sofia was thrown back through the air, landing with a thud on her back.

Jade gasped at her own sword, still not understanding how she had just done that. Sofia leapt up. Now she was furious. She struck at Jade again and again. Each time the pink sword connected with the blue ice-blade the same explosion happened and Sofia would end up on her back.

"Drop your sword and fight me with your hands!" Sofia challenged.

"No way!" Jade laughed which infuriated Sofia even more. She slammed the floor with her fist, sending out a devastating shock-wave of ice that sent Jade tumbling to the ground. Sofia wasted no time at all in leaping towards the defenceless Jade as her sword had slipped from her grip. Jade quickly rolled out of the way of the vicious strike, re-grabbing her pink sword. Jade swiped her blade against Sofia's, and the Ice-blade was thrown from her grasp.

"Yield!!!" Jade demanded.

Sofia stood silent with her fists clenched tightly down by her side. Her teeth gritted together wrathfully.

"Yield!!!!" Jade commanded again as she held the tip of her Pink sword to Sofia's throat.

"You'll have to strike me down!" Sofia's eyes raged as she leapt to the side, rolling away from Jade and reclaiming her Ice-blade.

"Impressive!" Linx complimented.

Sofia leapt back towards Jade, aggressively swinging her Ice-Blade. Jade dodged the attack and Sofia dropped her sword and placed her fingers to her head.

"What are you doing?" Jade asked with shock.

"I am a mind-fairy by nature!" Sofia roared.

Suddenly Jade dropped to her knees clutching her head and screaming.

"The mind is a fragile thing," Sofia growled as she picked up her Ice-blade and stepped towards Jade, holding the tip to her throat, "Yield!"

"NO!" Jade yelled as she grabbed her Pink sword. Sofia was stunned.

"How are you this strong?" Sofia gasped.

"I don't know!" Jade replied angrily as she stabbed Sofia through her shoulder, "Yield!"

Sofia yelped at the pain and then let out a long and frustrated sigh "I yield!"

"Looks like it's Jade versus Stacy in the final!" Linx announced excitedly.

"You had better win!" Sofia warned Jade as she marched off in a strop.

Stacy waited for Jade to step into the arena.

"I like your sword," she complimented.

"Thanks," Jade mumbled.

"Begin!" Linx roared.

Jade waited patiently for Stacy to stop fiddling with her manicured nails before finally the blonde-haired beauty glanced up through her long black eyelashes. She smiled and strutted towards Jade who gripped her pink sword tightly.

Stacy blew Jade a kiss like she had many other opponents, but her face tensed when nothing happened. Stacy frowned angrily as she clicked her fingers and again nothing happened.

"Why won't my magic work on you?!" Stacy gasped.

"I don't know," Jade shrugged as she took a step towards Stacy who for the first time today looked a little nervous. The blonde backpedalled away from Jade who pointed her pink sword at her throat, "Yield!"

Suddenly Stacy's worried and horrified expression changed to a smile.

"Silly girl!" Stacy giggled as she produced a glistening blue ice-blade. She swiped her sword aggressively and spitefully at Jade who blocked it nicely, despite being taken by surprise. There was no flashing pink explosion when Stacy's blade struck Jade's and Jade gulped as she blocked. Abruptly Stacy sliced her sword upwards, flinging Jade's blade from her grip.

"I don't need to ask you to yield, you'll yield when I stab you through the neck!" Stacy threatened scornfully.

Jade scrambled across the arena but Stacy had her cornered. I glanced around as I couldn't bare to watch. All of a sudden I spotted Reverend Crone muttering something under his breath and wiggling his fingers inconspicuously. *What was he doing?* Suddenly he turned and saw me. He winked at me with his scary one eye and grinned as he nodded his head towards the arena, signalling me to watch.

Stacy was about to stab her sword through a terrified Jade, when all of a sudden her heel snapped.

"Aghhhhhhhhh," she screamed as she fell to the floor clutching her swollen ankle. Jade rapidly scrambled across, grabbing her pink sword and held it to her face.

"Yield!" Jade yelled.

"I yie," Before Stacy could finish Jade stabbed her through the face.

"Sorry, didn't catch that in time," she said to Stacy smugly.

"Jade has won the tournament!!!" Linx roared.

Sofia ran up to Jade and hugged her tight.

"That was awesome!" She said.

"Thank you. Can we be friends now?" Jade asked.

Sofia regarded her for a second with a bewildered frown,

"Of course we can!" She grinned, "I'm sorry for being such a bitch. I'm working on it, ok!" She had a slight tear in her eye and Jade hugged her tight.

We all rushed up to Jade and congratulated her.

Miss Hoax made sure Stacy came back to life.

"I told you to remove those heels," Linx said smugly to her.

"Shut up Linx!" She groaned as she stomped off.

I ran up to Reverend Crone, "Did you do that?" I gasped.

He turned and smirked at me, "Do what?"

"You know? - The heel snap," I whispered.

"That was an act of God, my dear," he said smugly. Then he leant down close to my ear, "Besides, the little bitch deserved it," and with that he walked off.

Jade had been swept away with the crowd and celebrations as she went to receive her medal. So, I had begun heading back to my dorm, but I spotted Sofia heading towards the medical tent. I was concerned that she might be injured so rushed over, but I slowed my pace when I realised Tom was inside the tent. She hadn't spotted me so I discreetly watched and listened from outside as Sofia went inside.

Tom went to get up when he saw her but she shoved him back into his seat and climbed on top of him.

"What are you doing," he gasped nervously.

"Returning your kiss, I really didn't like it," she whispered seductively as her jaw wrapped around his passionately.

I bit my lip as I watched her eat his face excitedly as their lips merged together. I was so happy that Sofia finally gave in to her feelings. I felt a sort of gratitude and admiration for Tom, too. Fair play to him, he deserves this. I then decided I'd stuck around longer than I should have - I'm not a peeping-tom, *no pun intended,* so I took a leisured stroll back to my dorm, grinning all the way - so happy at witnessing such a happy moment – Sofia returning the kiss.

10- DARK SECRETS

As I walked back to my dorm and turned the corner, leaning against the wall and looking more like an Angel than anyone had a right to – was Lingwood.

"Hi," I mumbled. I couldn't think of anything else to say to him.

He grinned his crooked smile at me, stopping my breath and my heart. I couldn't imagine how even a Greek God could be anymore glorious. There was nothing about him that could be improved upon, apart from his constant blowing hot and cold with me –personality.

"I'm sorry for my behaviour this morning," he apologised.

I still wondered if he had any idea just how appealing his voice was - as smooth as velvet and as warm as trickling honey dripping into my ears.

"Why did you get so odd?" I asked.

He shrugged, "I like you," he admitted and I suddenly felt a little faint.

"Are you ok?" He asked, reaching out and grabbing my arm.

I suddenly forgot how to breathe as his golden eyes glared into mine. I felt a tinge of electricity surge through me as his cold skin touched mine.

"I'm fine," I wheezed, embarrassed as I knew I was blushing redder than a beetroot. "What do you mean you like me?" I choked out the words.

"Meet me later tonight about midnight," he instructed.

"Why?" I questioned, suddenly feeling a little nervous as my mind flashed back to what Vladimir had said. "You're a vampire, aren't you?" I gulped.

He slowly nodded.

"Are you going to eat me?" I panicked, despite finding my mind wondering to forbidden and naughty thoughts at him eating me. I frowned and hoped he didn't read my awful mind.

He smirked, "I would never eat you without your permission, Eleni," I wasn't sure if he *had* read my mind and that was an innuendo, or if he actually meant *eat* me. At this moment I wasn't sure which was worse.

"Your father said to me that you're toying with me," I blurted and then regretted it instantly.

Suddenly his expression changed to anger. "He shouldn't had done that!"

"It's ok. I trust you," I reassured, reaching out and grabbing his hand, worried that I had spoiled the mood. Clearly I had! He sighed and his face looked as though he were in agony.

"You are my rose, Eleni, and I am a thorn! Thorns hurt, stay away."

"But you just told me to meet you at midnight?" I said, trying not to sound too desperate.

"Yes, that was a mistake," he mumbled.

"Well, I'll be here! Right here where we are now, at midnight," I sulked as I crossed my arms in a strop. He found my tantrum very amusing.

"See you around, Eleni," he chuckled as he stepped away from me and into the shroud of shadows. – He had vanished.

I looked at the time and it was nearing 7.30pm. I gasped and rushed to the main hall where Reverend Crone instructed me to meet. The guards on the door stepped aside when they saw me, allowing me entry. Once inside I saw father standing alone at a table.

"Dad?" I called out.

"Welcome daughter," he said without even looking up.

I felt the rage rise up inside of me, but I took a few slow breaths and pushed it back down.

"Why am I here?" I demanded.

Now he *finally* looked up.

"A decision has been made to send you home to your farm to be with your mother."

I stood a little dumbfounded for a moment as I glared bewilderedly at him. "What?"

He let out a long sigh, "I felt we could train you, prepare you, but after watching your dismal performance in the tournament today, I realise I've left it too late. You should have been trained from a younger age and now as your father I need to protect you. Jealousaw is coming. If Linx and his team don't find some more stones tonight then he'll be here in two days. I can't risk you being here if-and when that happens. Stadley Hold has enough power to contain the situation and not allow him outside of these walls to terrorise the world, but we can't stop him from arriving here!"

"No, don't send me home father," I begged, "When is Linx going out to search for stones?"

"He leaves at 9pm!" Reverend Crone announced as he entered the room.

"She didn't need to know that information Joseph!" Father grumbled. "Don't even think about it sweetheart," Father pleaded as he looked at me.

"Oh I'm going with Linx," I stood firm.

"You can't even hold your own against a bloody basic Wood-fairy. She bested you within seconds of the fight starting. *My daughter* embarrassed and defeated within seconds!" Father sighed as he said it.

"Is that all you care about?!!!" I shouted, "Your stupid reputation!!!"

Reverend Crone was surprisingly quiet.

"What's the matter priest? No snide remark? No witty comeback?" Father snarled.

"Oh no Franklin, you're screwing this one up all by yourself," Reverend Crone sniggered mockingly.

Father then thumped the table making me jump. "You will obey me daughter. Pack your bags and I'll arrange transport for you tomorrow morning. I will not risk your life - my only child."

"You should have thought about that before you dragged me up here!" I spat back.

Suddenly Indira walked in, her soothing voice instantly calmed the room.

"Perhaps Eleni appears weak in your eyes because *we* are not allowing her to train to her full potential," she spoke to father.

"What do you mean?" Father barked, but even he found it hard to rage his wrath in Indira's calming and soothing presence.

"The *other* sword," Indira said firmly, but her voice was soft and always kind.

"If you are referring to 'The Time Realm Sword' then that is forbidden!" Reverend Crone growled, his voice wasn't soft – or kind.

Indira turned to face Reverend Crone, her wonderful unicorn-pastel hair flowing down to her perfect hips, "Reverend, we have to think of the greater good."

"Greater good my hairy arse cheeks. Time cannot be messed with! It is forbidden!!!" The Reverend argued.

"The Time-sword goes way beyond just time powers Josesph! You know this better than most!" Indira quarrelled, but her voice still never changed from its beautiful soft tone.

"ENOUGH!!!!" Father yelled with fury - plummeting the room into silence. "You are suggesting *my* daughter use 'The Burned

Soul's' sword. Cornelius fucking Strumple's own personal weapon! Have you lost your mind, Indira!"

"It called out to her," Indira reminded.

"Let me try, please father," I begged, turning fathers wrath towards me.

"That sword isn't *just* a 'Time Sword' Eleni. It is wielded by dark-magic - the darkest of magic ever to exist. I can't - I *will not*, allow my daughter to meddle with such a force that is so dangerous that even *we* daren't go near!"

"Then you may as well let Jealousaw in right now," Indira moaned, "I understand this sword better than all of you. Allow me to train her."

My eyes lit up at the prospect of Indira training me.

Reverend Crone snorted.

"Do you have something to say?" Indira turned sharply towards the Reverend, her usual peaceful and calm alluring voice had much more fire in it than usual.

"You may have had a fling with a 'Time Aristocrat' many moons ago, but do not be arrogant enough to think you can contain the dark magic that surrounds *this* sword!" Reverend Crone warned with a pointed finger.

"Jack was never a 'Time Aristocrat'," Indira's enchanting laugh echoed around the room.

"What do you mean?" Father and the Reverend both turned to face Indira, both with that same horrified and baffled expression on their faces.

"It is a story that I have allowed to go on for far too long now. It's time I let the truth have its day. *I* was 'The Time Aristocrat' that trapped Cornelius Strumple to the ends of the universe. I worshiped that man until Jack Mayers from Earth Realm Two, broke me from his spell," Indira almost purred as she reminisced.

"How can a simple human with no magical capabilities break you from such a powerful man's spell?" My father asked sceptically.

"The most powerful magic of all Franklin," Indira smirked.

"Love," Reverend Crone finished her sentence.

"Yes, Reverend, that is right. Only pure unconditionally raw true love can break any spell. But that's so rare that everyone forgets about it," Indira explained.

"It's so rare because we all lust and fall in and out of love so often nowadays that 'true love's power' has almost become a myth," Reverend Crone spoke. The priest now looked conflicted as though he were struggling with something. Reverend Crone after a few seconds of huffing and puffing finally piped up after clearly giving it some thought. "You are by far one of the most powerful Earth wizards to ever exist Franklin. Search your feelings. Make the right call!"

Father then let out a long sigh but didn't speak.

"Like you have all these years, Reverend!" Father snapped.

"Don't make this about me, Joseph!" The priest replied with a pointed finger.

"Tell us, Reverend Crone, why were you banished from all churches?" Father spat.

Reverend Crone smirked and said nothing.

"Tampering with prophesises and Holy books, wasn't it?" Father said strongly.

"And for being a drag queen on the weekends," the Reverend said with a wink, "Don't knock it until you've tried it," he cackled.

I couldn't help a giggle.

"He's *not* joking!" Father grumbled through squinted eyes.

"Reeeee-ally?" I gasped, half smirking and half in shock. I couldn't imagine a man who resembled 'Brendan Gleeson's' character in Harry Potter, 'Alastor *Mad Eye* Moody' in looks and personality, ever dressing up as a woman.

"I did it *one* time Miss Judge-ey," – *He rolled his eye* – "to piss off Pope John XIX back in the dark ages. Those *were* the days. Medieval times were good times for *real* men. Sword fights, punch ups and booze. I dressed up at his birthday party. I found it quite amusing to see the look on his face. It isn't a sin to express yourself! I'm still the toughest *sonofabitch* in the room, whatever clothing I'm wearing. As they found out when they tried to hang me for it, let me tell you now, that noose got nowhere near my neck. None of them were left standing *when I* walked out of that hall!" He grinned. "John XIX was said to have been killed by a mob of angry peasants, but there is no evidence to support this. It was less embarrassing for the church to come up with a story like that. The truth is I kicked all their arses and ended that fool!"

"You killed a Pope?" I gasped.

"Trust me, back in those days they were all frauds. Besides, it was self-defence," he winked.

"*I* will train her in the arts of time. Nobody knew 'The Burned Soul' better than me and if that sword has called out to Eleni, then it means she is the most powerful person in this room, possibly the universe!" Indira stated, changing the subject back to what mattered.

I puffed out my cheeks at *that* statement. This was a lot of pressure.

"So be it!" Father snarled as he stomped out of the room.

I followed him quickly into the other room, leaving Indira and Reverend Crone alone.

"Father!" I called out, stopping him in his tracks. "I won't let you down," I promised.

"I know you won't," he nodded sternly, "But Indira isn't the only one with secrets. I thought I could use you to defeat Jealousaw, but now I fear he'll sense who you are, and use *you* against me!"

"What do you mean?" I gasped.

His face became tormented and sad as he twisted it into sternness as though he was trying to hide his distraught, but I recognised the look. It was the same look I practiced in the mirror so often.

"Nothing daughter. Go get some rest. Your training with Indira will start tomorrow. God have mercy on us all," And with that he marched into his private chamber, bolting the door. Clearly he was hiding something!

Suddenly a loud alarm went off as the warning bells started ringing and Linx burst through the door like a-bat-out-of-hell. His dashing handsome features seemed concerned and frightened. The look of terror on his face resembled the first night I had met him when we hid from those demons.

"Sweepers are in the courtyard!!!" He yelled, his voice panic-stricken and trembling.

"GET HER OUT OF HERE!!!" Father emerged from the door, pointing at me.

"They've come for Jade, they've come for the chosen one. The prophesy!!!" Reverend Crone grunted.

"No, Reverend, they've come for Eleni," my father sighed.

"WHAT?" The Reverend barked.

"Now isn't the time Joseph. Get my daughter to safety!" Father ordered.

"And what about *you* Franklin?" Reverend Crone snarled.

"I'm going to destroy them once and for all!" He gritted.

"You can't. You'll use up too much energy from the stones and we need that energy to keep the shields strong so that Jealousaw can't get in!" Indira pleaded. "I need more time with Eleni. Don't do this Franklin. Let the Defenders do their job."

"What are Sweepers?" I begged for answers.

"You don't want to know, Eleni," Linx warned.

"NO!" I snapped. "You palmed me off with *that* last time. How it will give me nightmares. Well this entire compound is a nightmare that is next door to freaking Hell! So start talking!" I wasn't going to back down this time.

Linx sighed as he shared an uneasy look with my father. Reverend Crone, then, as he so often did, spoke up.

"They're dark creatures, widely considered to be one of the foulest to inhabit the wizarding world. Think Dementors from Harry Potter, only far worse. In the Potter world Dementors fed on human happiness and thus generated feelings of depression and despair in any person in close proximity to them."

Indira smirked towards the Reverend who raised an eyebrow.

"What?" He groaned, "I can enjoy a bit of fiction once in a while too ya know."

"I didn't say anything," she giggled.

"Anyway . . . Sweepers do all that too, but unlike Dementors in the Potter world, Sweepers main meal is feeding on a wizards potential. They hunger for that innocence. The higher the potential the more attracted they are to the wizard, or witch, or any magic-being. Once they feed on you for long enough, they suck all your abilities from you, even ones you haven't learnt yet. Now do you see our predicament?" The Reverend grumbled.

Suddenly the main doors flew open and three black Sweepers glided in. They were wraithlike and a thousand times worse than the Reverend had described.

They looked at me with glowing white eyes and whispered my name. "Eleni Sparkle."

I gulped as Indira pulled me away from their glare.

"Don't look into their eyes, Eleni," she warned.

"My surname is 'Fox!' Not Sparkle!" I mumbled to myself bewildered.

"It's your middle name," Father must have heard my mumble.

"Why would they call me by my middle name?" I asked.

Suddenly Reverend Crone slammed his Staff to the ground before father could answer.

"Be-gone demon," he yelled as a bright blue glow emerged from his staff.

The Sweepers shielded their eyes, cowering away from the light. "I've brought you some time, now get her out of here!" The Reverend screamed with fury.

"Take her up the mountain to the church," Indira instructed to Linx.

"But without Reverend Crone there, that's suicide," Linx protested.

"You are a stone chaser are you not? – Take her. Once you are inside the church it is holy-ground. You will be safe there!" Indira yelled, "NOW GO!"

As Linx dragged me away I looked over my shoulder to see father, Indira and Reverend Crone using their magic to trap the Sweepers. Loud demonic hisses and screams echoed down the corridor as we ran. Linx grabbed his walkie-talkie as he tugged my arm as I struggled to keep pace with him.

"This is Stone Chaser One. The Stone chaser team must commence up the mountain without myself or Reverend Crone," he ordered.

"That's suicide boss," the handheld radio spoke back.

"We haven't a choice. The stones are running low. This is what we've trained for men!" Linx barked, trying to ignite some passion and motivation in them, despite knowing deep in his heart that they were probably all going to die.

"Yes sir. Commencing up the mountain now," the radio squawked.

"Happy hunting," Linx said to the Walkie before strapping it back to his belt. He let out a deep sigh, knowing he's just more than likely sent them to their death.

"You too sir," It fizzled.

We ran outside of the main hall and more warning bells sounded. A man ran past us screaming, "Demons!!!"

Linx grabbed his radio again as we hid behind a small bush.

"This is Linx to main gate, what's going on?"

The radio crackled a response, *"Breaches are everywhere!"*

"Shit!" Linx sighed to me. "The stones are weakening and the demons can sense it – Come on, we have to get to the church."

"Thought you'd never ask," I flirted and then frowned at my own words. Now really wasn't the time to let my hormones take over!

He glared a confused look my way and then returned my smirk, "Stay focused!"

"I'm scared!" I retaliated.

"I know Little E, me too. We have to go!"

"Not without my friends!" I stood with my arms folded.

He let out a long angry sigh, "We don't have time for this!"

"I'm not going without them!" I stood my ground.

His blue eyes with tresses of green swirling within them suddenly trapped me. My eyes fused with his and despite his gorgeous glare making me go weak at the knees, I remained strong and didn't blink, as I begun to frown. He instantly frowned back and usually I would certainly lose this contest, but I thought of my friends.

"I could waste time arguing with you, but you're clearly your father's daughter! Lead the way!" He groaned with despair, but still not breaking eye contact with me.

Finally, I buckled and blushed and glanced away from his mouth-watering stare, unlocking my eyes from his deep magnetic pull.

I sighed louder than I had meant to as I found myself back in that triangle of who I liked more. When I was with Lingwood I'd think it's him and when I was with Indira I was adamant it was her. And now here I was with Linx and my mind changed once again.

We darted into the dorm corridor and headed towards our dorm rooms. Suddenly father's voice came on the speakers, echoing around the school.

"THIS IS HEADMASTER FRANKLIN FOX. ALL STUDENTS REPORT IMMEDIATELY TO THE MAIN HALL!"

Linx turned and glared at me.

"This is *really* serious. Main hall protocol is only for when the school is getting completely overrun!"

Sofia suddenly burst out of the room, nearly colliding with us. She was smirking and glowing.

"You're out-of-character-happy," Linx joked.

"I am very happy in fact, thank you. Do you guys know what is going on?" She beamed and I raised an eyebrow at her chirpiness.

Suddenly Tom shuffled out of the room behind her.

"Tom, what are you doing here?" Linx asked, and then the penny dropped, "OH," he smirked as he looked at Sofia and then back at Tom.

"Tom was just . . . err . . . helping me with some homework," Sofia gulped awkwardly.

"Yes, that's right, homework," Tom agreed as he went a little red.

"Bet you were studying *real hard*," Linx chuckled and Tom burst out laughing and then quickly stopped as Sofia glared angrily at him.

"We need to go!" Linx suddenly remembered, "Your friends will be safer in the main hall, all the wizards and witches will be there, but *we need* to leave!"

"I agree, but why wouldn't we be safer there too?" I asked.

"Because Little E, The Sweepers are after potential, and you have bundles of it apparently," he winked with a cheeky smirk. I rolled my eyes and smirked back.

Suddenly my heart sank, "What about Jade?"

"I'll take care of her," Sofia promised with a beaming smile as she gripped me in a hug. "NOW GO!" She ordered.

"Ok," I sighed, it was so nice to see Sofia this happy.

"Stay safe bro," Linx said as he shook Tom's hand.

"You too," he replied firmly. "I *will not* let no harm come to any of your friends," he stated with determined grit as he looked me deep in the eyes. Tom was a good man.

I nodded.

"He's so cute when he tries to act all manly and tough," Sofia whispered to me and we both giggled, causing the guys to look up at us. "Come on my Knight in shining armour, let's go!" Sofia groaned sarcastically to Tom and they both hurried off down the corridor.

"She seems so happy," I said to Linx.

"She clearly just needed a shag," he chuckled as we hurried off in the opposite direction.

"Linx!" I protested with a playful slap to his very firm arm, "Sofia wouldn't make things *that* easy for Tom. Trust me on that one."

"Yeah, Sofia's not an easy catch, but I doubt she's *that* happy from just a kiss. The heat of the moment, a split second of forgetfulness as you get caught up in the many emotions of lust, *anything* can happen – think about it," Linx's blue-green eyes gazed into mine and I lost all chain of thought as I *did* think about it.

I quickly blushed and tried to avert my eyes before he noticed my-no-doubt-tomato-red-face. *OH* – I fretted as I suddenly realised I was looking at his crotch. My eye's now darted left and right and no doubt panic was flared all over my face as I so obviously tried to look anywhere but at him.

"Are you ok?" He asked, clearly sensing my blush.

Every time he spoke, it affected me in forbidden ways. My heart skipped a beat as I composed myself and my embarrassment.

"Yes. I'm fine," I gulped. "We had better pick up the pace," I quickly suggested.

"Agreed!" He said with a nod as he strode on ahead. I slowed my pace deliberately to study him for a moment. He looked like all the statues of Gods that littered textbooks – with his chiselled abs visible through his black vest-top and bulging everywhere else . . . and I mean *everywhere* else. My eyes almost flicked to his firm buttocks and back to his crotch – suddenly, he turned around, almost catching me checking him out. I seemed to lose all sense around him.

"Come on Little E, keep up. We *have* to get moving!" He called back with that cheeky-boyish crooked smile that I loved so much. My heart picked up its pace and my legs almost went to jelly, but I rapidly obeyed his command and caught up with him. We dashed out into the open courtyard that would usually be buzzing with students. Now it was eerily quiet and abandoned. I went to say something and he speedily shoved his hand over my mouth, forcing me against the wall as he placed his finger up to his lips to hush me. I gulped as a grunting and hissing sound bundled past us.

He slowly took his warm hand down from my mouth and then I noticed our bodies were touching. I could feel his hot breath mixing with mine and for a split second we were trapped in each others gaze. I could sense he wanted to kiss me, as I did him, but he resisted this urge, and to my frustration he pulled away.

We snuck across the courtyard in silence as we both contemplated the coming horror, until we reached the main back gate. There were no guards on it this time, unlike last time when Stephanie had to distract them. The weather was eerily silent, misty and cold. Linx grabbed a rucksack that was hidden behind a tree.

"What's that?" I whispered.

"Every stone chaser keeps an emergency clothing and first aid bag hidden around these parts. You just never know when you're going to need them," he nodded.

We headed through the gate. We tried to desperately stay as silent as we could - the gate creaked as we opened it and walked through, echoing around the soundless compound. Just as I got outside the compound something grabbed me from behind, ripped at my collar and tore the fabric. I ducked and spun in panic and kicked hard. Linx leapt back just as startled as me. This creature was, was a . . .

"HELLBIE!!!!" Linx screamed as he pushed the gate shut to prevent it from entering Stadley Hold, sealing us outside the compound with this thing! It was big, bigger and heavier than me by quite a few kilos. Black fluid ran down the front of its sandy-coloured shirt. Linx rapidly jumped between me and the monster, jamming his knife between its ribs, burying it to the hilt. – But this thing kept coming. Linx's knife now protruded from its chest. A scrap of my collar, which was clenched between its teeth, dropped as its lower jaw snapped open. A ghastly growl emerged from its open mouth as it lunged at me. Linx had drawn his sword and with one clean swipe, sliced it's head clean off.

"W, w, was tha-that a Zombie?" I hyperventilated.

"Yes!" He clarified, "A Hell-Zombie. We call them Hellbies. Although some people back in the day called them 'Dombies,' which stands for demonic zombie," Linx sounded as terrified as I was. "We haven't seen one of them in a long, long time," he gulped.

I suddenly burst out crying and just couldn't stop. Stupid traitorous tears, this was embarrassing. All of a sudden a firm grip cradled me in a strong embrace. It was warm - and all the agitation dissolved as soon as I looked up at his face. Calmness swept over me and I suddenly felt safe. My tears dried up and I breathed a sigh of relief.

"Don't cry, Little E. You're safe now. I've got you," he comforted and reassured me.

I squeezed him tight and never wanted to let go. Suddenly his grip loosened.

"We have to get going. Hellbies rarely come just one. They'll be a herd heading this way no doubt," he warned.

I gulped as we slowly untangled our arms. I looked up into his eyes and he looked down into mine and smiled.

"Let's get to church!" He said and I nodded in agreeance and we begun to make our way up the mountain. It was dark, creepy, and constantly misty. The silence was terrifying as we crunched through the foliage of the woods. The nearer we got to the church the colder it got - but we both felt hot from the fast-paced march that we had kept up hill through the mud and dirt. It had become almost muggy under the ceiling of trees and dark clouds. I pulled off my sweater and knotted it around my waist and saw that he had ripped his vest deliberately at the top to give that unbuttoned affect – *not as a fashion statement* – it was getting toasty. Or was that me just having a hot flush? His stubbly neck flowed down to his masculine chiselled chest. His perfect musculature no longer merely hinted at behind his tight fitted vest. Now I could see the top of his chest muscle and I tried not to drool – oh he was yummy! He stared at me, bewildered by my tortured expression and I had to think fast on my feet when he asked if I was alright. I quickly pretended I had lost my nerve.

"What if I lose you and get lost?" I think he bought it.

"We'll never lose each other," he said and I wasn't sure if he meant to say it as passionately as I heard it. My lips parted in gasp as my heart melted.

"Keep up!" He ordered as he walked on ahead, holding the damp ferns and webs of moss aside for me. The path curled up through darker trees and I could sense eyes watching us from the shadows. He helped me over the fallen trees and boulders, lifting me by my elbow and then releasing me instantly when I was clear. His warm touch, although so different from Lingwoods cold touch, still was equal in its shuddering affect on me – never failing to make my heart thud erratically. Ignited by his touch my eyes took on a life of their own. I desperately tried to keep my focus away from his perfection as much as I could, but it wasn't possible, and each time I took a peek his stunning-looks pierced straight through me.

At first, the trees were spread apart, but the deeper we went, the more clustered they became. Moonlight trickled through the trees, casting long shadows. Suddenly a branch snapped a few yards away from us. I instantly froze solid with terror, scanning the area rapidly, so did Linx momentarily, but then he pushed on and dragged me with him.

"We are being hunted," he whispered, "We have to keep going!"

My head twisted around at the darkness that hugged this place and suddenly that chill in the air returned alongside the chilling-silence.

"Eleni!" Linx broke me out of my fearful trance. "There is a hundred and fifty acres of woods out here. We are not alone and we have to keep moving forwards no matter what!"

My breathing quickened and every instinct in my body told me to move slowly, but Linx dragged my arm and we hurried through the forest as another branch snapped behind us, closer than before.

Every rational thought left me and I ran harder than I ever had in my entire life. The leaves and twigs crunched under our weight as we both sprinted towards the small church which we could just about see in the distance now. Another twig snapped behind me, but I couldn't bring myself to turn around. Linx told me not to stop as it would slow us down, so I listened. We were hell-bent on getting to this damn church and we were so close now. Suddenly my feet slipped on the leaves and I slid a few inches before landing hard on my knees. I made a slight yelp sound and Linx glanced back at me, causing him not to see the outstretched tree root protruding from the ground. I had stumbled to my feet as I heard another noise behind me, but Linx clutched his ankle in pain.

"Keep going!!!" He urged me from the ground. "Get to the church! Leave me!!!" He ordered.

I shook my head and dragged him up, this was one order I wasn't going to obey.

I could feel the waves of infuriated disapproval rolling off of him, but I wasn't sure if it was because I had ignored his command, or if it was aimed at himself. I placed my arm around his waist and hoisted him along. He placed his arm around my shoulder and we hopped and staggered down the thin path leading to the church. Another noise came from behind us and I couldn't make out what it was and this time I instinctively glanced back. Pure terror coursed through my body, and when I didn't see anything behind me, my fear went into overdrive. It was closing in on us fast and I feared that whatever was hunting us didn't want to be seen until it was good-an-ready. We were so close now, inches from the holy-land where nothing demonic of evil could cross. We could see the brightness ahead.

A black shadow as quick as a flash, scorched past me in a blur and we could just about make out a dark figure suddenly blocking our path to the holy-ground.

I struggled to hold Linx's weight and we nearly fell as I became immobile with fear.

The figure slowly walked towards us and I soon realised that it was a person. His long black hair matched his long black coat that blew in the wind around his colourless chalk features.

"Vladimir!" Linx gasped.

"Hello dog," his voice hissed as he eyed Linx.

Then his head twisted to me, "Hello Eleni."

"Hi," I gulped.

"What brings you out here on such a foul night," Vladimir questioned.

"We are heading to the church," I replied, "Now if you'll excuse us, I must get Linx there, as he needs to rest on safe ground."

Vladimir's eyes were a deep burgundy colour that was disturbing and sinister. His sharp eyes opened widely as he glared towards Linx.

"Ahhhh yes, you are injured," he wavered his arm in a gesture for us to pass.

As we walked past I noticed in the corner of my eye Vladimir's blood-red lips part, his teeth were fang-like and unnaturally white like sticks of chalk. His nostrils flared and a feral snarl ripped from his throat. This was the single most frightening noise I had ever heard, and cold chills ran from the crown of my head to the back of my heels. All of a sudden without warning Linx shoved me to the side, I hadn't seen him get his sword out, but he had it ready in hand. The sharp metal sword pierced straight through the menacing Vladimirs neck. The fiend dropped to his knees and Linx yanked the sword free. "Come on, quick!" Linx urged as he hopped on one leg.

I was almost rendered to the ground, rooted in place, terrified into absolute immobility. Linx had to grip my elbow and yank me sharply to break my trance, and even then he was fortunate I snapped out of it, as he wouldn't have had the strength to carry me thanks to his twisted ankle. I staggered up from the mud and we embraced as we hobbled across the slippery sludge. I glanced over my shoulder to see Vladimir slowly rising. I was so stunned with fear that I nearly forgot how to walk, fortunately Linx and I helped each other shuffle and stagger towards the church.

Suddenly, I heard Vladimirs sharp breathing behind me and the sickening growl. I felt him grab my shoulder and I froze with terror, but his hand snapped back and released its grip as though something had shocked it. I twisted on my heel sharply and he was a few inches from my face, causing me to startle backwards. My breath caught in my throat and I gasped with panic. His sinister red eyes were so dark that they were almost completely black. His inhuman blood-red lips snarled a set of chilling white fangs, but he didn't take another step towards me. Frustration radiated over his pale features.

"He can't get you, Eleni. We are on holy soil now," Linx sounded almost teasing and smug as he said it.

I looked around at my surroundings. We were in a small - perfectly round meadow, filled with amazing wildflowers of all colours. Yellow, violet, soft whites and light blues. I could hear the trickling lullaby of a bubbling stream that drizzled in-an-around the rocks like soft soothing music. A sense of calmness fell over this place like a blanket dropped from a high window, slowly floating down to enwrap the objects safely that were underneath it. This blanket had embraced me now, and I felt my fear seep away. I looked up and frowned as I noticed a haze of butterfly sunlight spreading out over us. I glared down at my watch, it was 9.30pm.

"How is the sun shining?" I gasped.

"The days are a lot longer over the holy-land," Linx clarified. I thought nothing could surprise me now after everything I had seen so far since coming to Stadley Hold – but, I was clearly mistaken. Seeing Vladimir a few inches from me standing in the dark with the moonlight seeping through the trees - and then me standing in direct sunlight, was surreal. Night literarily met day directly above me.

I had wanted to question Vladimir, but I just couldn't bear to face him – he looked so terrifying. I shielded my gaze from his dead-eyes, - they were like Sharks eyes and I had to just get away. I walked, awestruck at the beauty and welcomed the distraction, through the soft grass and swaying flowers. The warm gilded air hugged my body, taking away all my fright from the evil that was behind me. I looked up and could see the small church. We were here and finally safe - although my mind couldn't help but think of the Sweepers and Vladimir waiting for us, but what stayed on my mind the most was father's reactions, did he too, have dark secrets?

11- *Little-sister-zoned!*

We were inside the church now and finally out of sight from that creature Vladimir. Linx plonked himself down on one of the benches, clutching his swollen ankle.

"You need to ice that," I pointed out the obvious.

"Yes. Check Reverend Crones personal chamber, he's sure to have a beer fridge in there somewhere," Linx urged.

I nodded and walked through a small wooden door.

"For a priest he's not very . . ." I paused searching for the right word, but Linx understood what I was getting at and answered me "Yes. He's an unusual man, but nonetheless a great man."

"Oh really?" I called out from the room as I scanned my surroundings, glancing at a small messy bed and a few scattered clothes, cigarette buds and empty beer bottles, until my eyes clamped onto the small fridge and freezer in the corner of the room. "I assumed you two didn't like each other."

"Reverend Crone has a dry sense-of-humour, very sarcastic and insulting, but underneath all that he has a heart of gold" Linx explained. "He guided me and helped me a lot to grow into the man I am today. He looked out for me after my parents died."

"Fair enough," I replied as I chucked him a cold beer and some ice.

"You read my mind," he smirked cheekily.

He looked so manly and handsome just sitting there with his foot up and guzzling back a beer coolly.

The chains on the big doors to Hell rattled and a few ghostly howls escaped. I glanced back with dread.

"Don't worry. I'll protect you from the devil," he promised.

I looked back at him and his eyes were inviting me to come and sit next to him.

"My hero," I muttered.

"Better get comfy Little E, we may be here a while. Oh and don't tell Reverend Crone that I am drinking his stash," Linx chuckled.

"Only if I can have some," I teased.

He raised a mischievous eyebrow.

"Usually I'd be the responsible one and claim that one of us underage drinking is bad enough, but given what you've just been through with 'The Sweepers', dodging demons and nearly getting eaten by that Hellby and then a vampire, I think one beer wouldn't hurt – but, don't tell your father! Or anyone, in fact!"

"Well, it's not our fault that we are trapped in a church with nothing else to drink. Reverend Crone has nothing else here," I shrugged with a naughty smirk as I grabbed a beer from the fridge.

"With me being twenty, if we were in England right now, what I am doing wouldn't be considered a crime, but out here the legal age is twenty-one," he rolled his eyes.

"It's not so bad for you, but I'm *only* seventeen," I grimaced after I had said it, regretting reminding him of our age gap!

"Yes. One drink is all I am allowing you!" He instructed seriously, but his smirk remained.

I casually sat myself down next to him and took a sip from the beer. He watched me intently as I swallowed, laughing as I pulled a face of disgust.

"First beer, I take it?" He sniggered.

"Well, *I am* only seventeen!" I replied – *why did I just remind him of the age gap again?!!!!!* I clenched my fist unseen from him by my side as I gritted my teeth.

"Such a rebel," he teased as he took a huge sip.

"Shut up," I giggled as I playfully slapped his firm arm.

He turned and looked at me with a crooked smile.

"Cheers," he said as he clonked his beer bottle with mine and then took another swig.

"Cheers," I repeated his words.

"You're supposed to drink after you cheers," he chuckled.

"Oh," I said a little embarrassed, "I know, I just waited a second that's all," I lied and then took a bigger swig than I had meant to and nearly choked. He saw straight through my bluff of course.

"Riiiiight," he laughed, "You choked because you lied. That's God punishing you for lying to me."

"Oh really?" I groaned with despair.

"Yes, really," he laughed radiantly.

"And what's the punishment for underage drinking?" I teased as I poked my tongue out at him - the beer clearly already going to my head.

"I don't think the lord would want us to die of thirst," he shrugged with a crooked grin, "Besides, there really is nothing else to drink here. You said it yourself. Reverend Crone doesn't even have a water tap."

"Can't argue with *that* reasoning," I whispered with an inviting smile.

I glared at his eyes for a moment and his beauty stunned my mind. I blinked and looked away, taking another swig to hide my blush.

"Grab us another one, please," he asked as he clonked his empty beer bottle down on the wooden bench next to him.

My eyes bulged as I still had plenty left in my bottle. I nodded and quickly downed the rest of mine to catch up with him.

Linx frowned at me, "Easy-tiger," he warned.

"Like you said, there is nothing else to drink," I shrugged as I walked into the other room, trying to hide my slight stagger.

This time I grabbed a few bottles to save me from going back and forth.

"I hope they're all for me," he protested, but I had already begun swigging one of them.

"Seriously, take it easy Little E," he pleaded.

I nodded and obeyed, slowing my sip.

"The last thing I need with my damaged ankle is to have to look after your drunken arse! Or clean up your puke," he said seriously to me, but his playful smirk told me that this wasn't a demand, but a polite request. I respected him for treating me like an adult and not a kid and it was cute that he cared.

"But what if this is my last night on earth?" I asked as a tear somehow appeared in my stupid eye!

He turned to me - shock and horror spread over his gorgeous face as he shuffled up on the bench closer to me. Our bodies now touched and I trembled as he placed his arm around my shoulder. "Why would you say that, Little E?" He asked softly.

"Vladimir is waiting outside for us. Demons and zombies stalk the woods that surround us. We have Jealousaw waiting to land here and kill us. The magic-stones are weak. Why wouldn't I assume that this could be my last night?"

I bowed my head; I couldn't believe I was crying. What a pathetic idiot. God knows what he must think of me. I tried to hide my sob but he spotted the traitorous tears drizzling down my cheek.

"Don't cry Little E," he hugged me tight and his citrus scent filled my nose, causing my brain to short-circuit. He cupped my cheek, wiping away the tears. His warm touch made my pulse rise.

"I'm fine!" I lied as I tried to hold onto what little pride I had left after humiliating myself here. "Look, I don't need your pity!" I suddenly said firmly. I was surprised at my own sharpness; I was almost rude the way I had snapped. God I sounded like Sofia! I hadn't meant it, but I think my own anger at myself had seeped out and attacked him.

"Is that what you think this is?" He gently grasped my arm and spun me to face him.

I could see that I had taken him by complete surprise at that outburst and the thought that I could have hurt him consumed me "I'm sorry," I blubbered like a moron.

"Why would you think that?" His incredible eyes gazed into mine and I almost lost all chain of thought.

"I know my father is headmaster, but I don't want you to feel obliged. I can take care of myself," I sucked in a breath, forcing myself to loosen my tight clutch that I had on my humility. "I do really appreciate it though," I backpedalled slightly, "But like I said, I can take care of myself!" I clarified again bluntly. He frowned with what I think was disappointment.

"Of course you can look after yourself Little E, and there is absolutely no reason to pity you," his eyes fused with mine and I found myself in a trance. "This has nothing to do with your dad. I know it sounds bonkers, but all I want to do is take care of you."

I shot a bewildered glare and had already blurted the word "Why?" before I could take it back. My entire body was on alert now, desperate to hear his reasoning. He looked deep into my eyes and licked his lips before he spoke and I found my gaze dropping to his mouth, wondering what he tasted like.

"There is just something about you Little E," he whispered, "Something I can't and don't want to shake."

His blue-ish-green tinted eyes lightened and the stubble on his chin glistened as it reflected the sun that shun in through the stained-glass-window. I suddenly couldn't breathe as my entire heart froze. Everything inside me wanted to kiss him. I found myself leaning in, feeling our connection too. Suddenly my heart pounded in my ears and my tummy was twisted in knots as it roiled with anticipation. Right when his full sexy lips were inches from mine, he suddenly pulled back. "You're like a little sister to me. That's why I feel so protective of you." My head jolted back as though someone had slapped me. Embarrassment bolted through me like lightening.

"Of course," I gulped back my gasp of shame. "You're like a brother to me too," I shot a rapid response as I took a huge swig of beer to hide my humiliating flushed face. More traitorous tears left my bloodshot eyes without my permission. I've seen people friendship-zoned before and that *must* hurt, but the pain I felt right now was the worst I could imagine. My wounded heart throbbed as though someone was stabbing it over and over. Oceans of tears were building up and up ready to flood out like an unstoppable tidal-wave. My pride was hurt, my emotions were running wild and I felt I had reached an all time low. I was embarrassed and humiliated at the hurtful rejection I felt, I longed for him and he didn't for me. The shame I felt for misreading the signals made me want to punch myself in the face. How stupid I had been to assume I stood a chance with him. Women like Stacy and Indira would be in his league. He was in the high divisions and I was in the bottom leagues. I couldn't even be friendship zoned, I wasn't even important enough in this mans life to be considered as a friend. I had been placed in a worse place than friendship-zoned.

I had just been little-sister-zoned.

12- A DEAL WITH A DEVIL

I woke up with my head nestled into Linx's lap. I was half mortified that I had fallen asleep on him, and the other half of me content. He didn't know I was awake and I didn't want him to know, as I was enjoying feeling him slowly trickle his fingers through my hair. I almost purred like a cat being stroked, but remained silent not wanting to give away that I was conscious. I had a sob and he made me laugh and then a few beers later I had forgotten all about my sadness and just enjoyed his company. I don't even remember passing out, but here I was on his warm lap.

His radio suddenly bleeped and he gently nudged himself across, easing me slowly onto the bench, taking great care not to wake me as he slid my head from his lap, cradling my cranium with his hands until my head was securely and softly placed onto the cold wooden bench. I felt his warm smooth lips press against my forehead as he kissed my head.

"Sleep tight Little E," he whispered.

I opened my eyes very slightly into thin slits to not give away that I was awake. I kept my eyes concealed under my lashes as I peeked to see where he had gone. Linx walked into the other room and I could hear him on his Walkie-talkie.

"What do you *mean* you can't locate anymore stones?" He gasped into the radio.

"They're located too deep within the mountains, boss. There aren't enough of us. We've taken heavy casualties already!" – The radio fizzed.

"You are a Stone Chaser!" Linx barked angrily, "The entire castle relies on us!"

"I'm sorry boss. There are too many demons protecting them. We can't get to them!" – The radio crackled.

"God-damn it!" Linx yelled as he threw down the Walkie-talkie.

I couldn't pretend I was asleep any longer as I got up and walked in, "What is it?" I asked, making out I hadn't heard the conversation.

"Nothing," he sighed.

"Didn't sound like nothing," I folded my arms.

He hesitated for a moment, debating if he should tell me the truth or not.

"Most of the Stone Chaser team have been wiped out. The ones that are left can't get to the stones due to there being too many demons. I can't help them because Vladimir has us trapped inside this blasted church!" He kicked the chair in anger.

"Can't you radio the castle for help?" I suggested.

"Oh I never thought of that!" He moaned sarcastically.

"Hey!" I growled.

"Sorry," he apologised, "The castle aren't responding."

I suddenly felt engulfed in fear and dread. I hoped that Sofia, Dotty, Stephanie, Estella and Jade were ok. I hoped dad was ok, despite my dislike for the man, and then my mind went to Lingwood and Indira.

"We need to get back there!" I urged.

"And do what?" Linx snorted.

"And help them!" I yelled.

"With my swollen ankle we wouldn't make it half way down the mountain without getting picked off – and, besides, Vladimir has us cornered," Linx made valid points.

"How do we kill a vampire?" I suddenly asked.

"A wooden stake to the heart paralyzes them but doesn't kill them. Once they are rendered immobile by the wooden Stake, you need to then cut off their head completely from their body. Only then can a powerful wizard or witch send their spirit back to hell," Linx explained. "And if you don't do all of that, then after a while the wooden stake becomes useless and they will locate their head and place it back on. Once it is placed back with its body then their neck will heal and they'll be back to normal."

"Can't a witch or a wizard kill a vampire with just magic?" I asked.

"There are very few wizards, warlocks, or witches with the capability to do that. It takes a great deal of power, a power that very few possess," Linx explained.

"What if I shoved him onto holy soil?"

"Any unholy creature no matter how powerful, will burn to dust if they step foot on Holy land. But there is no way you'd be able to do it - and don't even *think* about trying!" He warned.

"To get us out of here and help our friends, I have to try!" I insisted.

"Bullshit!" He snapped. "You aren't going anywhere. It's too dangerous to try!"

"I WILL DO THIS TO SAVE MY FRIENDS, LINX!!!!" I shouted angrily and loudly, "EVEN IF I HAVE TO MAKE A DAMN DEAL WITH THE DEVIL TO DO IT!!!!!"

Suddenly the room went black and I couldn't see Linx anymore. It was as if I were floating in black water. I couldn't see anything, no floor, no ceiling, no walls, just blackness.

"Linx!!!!" I cried out. "LINX!!!!!"

But nothing.

All of a sudden I could see Sofia screaming as Tom got eaten alive by a demon. Dotty tried to run but she got eaten too. Jade was crying and Stephanie tried to hold them back but there were too many of them. – Demons were everywhere!

Then the image faded and I heard a whisper in my ear, "This hasn't happened yet."

"Who said that?" I gasped with fear as I jolted my head in all directions, as panic seized my body in a tight grip.

The wind suddenly picked up, howling like a wolf under the moonlight. All of a sudden the wind stopped and there was complete silence. It was so quiet you could have heard a pin drop.

I was now outside on the grass, outside the church. Dramatically as I turned around I was startled by a skinny man in the shadows. He seemed to have greyish-dirty-white skin, long dark brown greasy curly hair, and scary dark soulless eyes. This nasty looking character was wearing a sort of reddish black coloured long coat with a huge collar. The material was rigid and scale like as if it was made out of crocodile skin and thick leather. Underneath his long coat was a brown tunic with a fancy snakeskin leather waistcoat with some sort of armour on it. He was wearing long black leather boots that stopped exactly on the kneecaps - shaped in a sharp pointed spear as it covered his patellas.

"What is going on!!!" I screamed. "Come out from the shadows! Where are my friends? I demand you show them to me? Are they alright? What was that?" I cried.

"It's rude to demand you know, dearest," the guy said in a soft but ascorbic voice that was like acid on the ears and sent chills down my spine.

I suddenly thought back to Indira's warning the other night, when I was out to dinner with her. How she said that 'The Burned Soul' would reach out to me.

"Are you Cornelius Strumple?" I guessed. My voice jittered as I was terrified and so nervously unnerved.

He raised his eyebrow as though he were surprised at my guess.

"In the flesh," the melodramatic man screeched rather sudden as if he were excited in a high pitch hiss. He spoke prim and proper but with an icy undertone as he stepped forwards and took a dramatic bow. Then he glanced up from his bowed position gazing with his huge black pupils and snarled, showing his rotten yellowish green teeth.

"Now what do you want?" He hissed in a serious and intimidating acidic voice.

"Want?" I gulped.

"Yes dear. Think about what you just said. Now, how badly do you want to throw that Vampire into this" . . . He paused for affect before grinning . . . "*Holy* land," he gasped, placing his nails to his mouth as though he were biting them in fear. He then removed his hand and sniggered.

"How are you here on this holy land?" I gasped.

He tapped his nose, "Holy land can't stop me getting inside your head. I know I said I'm here in the flesh, but that may have been a slight lie. Perhaps I should confess as we are in a church after all," he laughed.

"Are my friends alright?" I begged.

"*That* was a vision you saw of what may or may-not happen in the near future. Now you know who I am and what I do, I take it?" He snarled.

I gulped my fear down and decided I wouldn't be afraid.

"Yes, I heard you are someone who gets people what they want," I replied, trying desperately to hide my terror.

"Depends what it is that they want, dearest," the man's curdling voice said as he stepped a little closer to me.

I begun, "I want -"

"- Ahh, a woman that knows what *she* wants, I always admire a woman that knows what *she* wants. It's rare ya know!" He pointed his finger with a chuckle. "First though, how did *you* acquire *my* name?" Cornelius Strumple asked, interrupting me midsentence whilst turning his head to one-side, still gawking at me with those dreadful dark eyes.

I gulped again but composed my fear.

"That's not important, now can you help me or not?" I bluffed my confidence but still couldn't remove the slight alarm in my voice.

Cornelius, still with his head titled sideways, smiled, then straightened his neck and said as he theatrically and confidently walked towards me and then past me, "Of course, all business and no play. What is it *you* desire dear girl?" He turned rather suddenly and quick as he stood behind me and whispered chillingly into my ear, leaning in so close that I could feel his icy breath on my neck.

"Only your services," I responded, trying so desperately to sound tough and as though I wasn't completely and utterly terrified.

"Well, *that's* rather *obvious* isn't it, otherwise you wouldn't be speaking to me," Cornelius sarcastically said, as he let out an uneasy short spine-tingling snigger, that made my hair stand on end.

"I want to help my friends!" I gulped, already regretting this.

"Helping another, how noble, but then that's what you church goers are all about, aren't ya. I take it your friend who we mustn't speak of, the one whom you acquired my name but you won't tell, I take it he or she told you that I don't *just* do," Cornelius giggled. He paced around me in a sort of rally with his hands placed behind his back whilst looking down at the floor.

"Yes, she told me you are a deal maker," I announced.

"So, it was a *she* that told you my name," he mumbled in an evil tone. Cornelius then stopped in his tracks, seizing his march, but still gazing at the floor with his head down. Suddenly he rapidly looked up, turning his head to its side and smiled a sickening grin.

"Unfortunately for you my dear girl, a negotiation requires two interested parties, and I'm sure you have nothing that could possibly interest me. On the other hand though, my sweet, sweet heart can't allow such a noble request to sail on by," Cornelius sniggered in a vile voice.

"So you'll help them then?" I asked with a lit up face.

"Well, I didn't quite say *that!*" He replied as he turned speedily, looking into my eyes, destroying the lit up expression on my face. "I'll go to your friends and offer, errm, let's say assistance. What happens from there is their choice. Sofia,

Stephanie, Dotty, Estella. Anyone I missed? Oh, mustn't forget dear old Linx," he giggled sadistically.

"How could you know their names?" I gasped as coldness embraced my body, sending chills up and down my spine.

"I am a man that just knows. So, forget your friends for a moment. What is it you actually *truly* want my dear child? First kiss? Lose your virginity? Or is it less selfish and boring, like save your friends?" He faked a yawn. "Or, to kill the Vampire that haunts the town folk, Vladimir?" Cornelius sniggered. "Could *you* possibly leave dear old heartthrob Lingwood without a father though? Perhaps the apple hasn't fallen far from the tree with you, if *you* . . . got the guts," he snarled as he said it, protruding his lips into a hideous smile.

"Or perhaps, you'd like me to whip up a love potion for you and Linx. Nothing worse than being the little sister," he twirled his hand in the air melodramatically before looking at me with a wide grin.

"How do you know all this?" I wheezed with panic.

"What? Know you're a virgin and never even kissed a guy?" Cornelius sniggered. "It's not hard to figure out. You grew up on an isolated farm with horses and were homeschooled by good-old mummy. Of course your innocence is intact," he giggled and I blushed with embarrassment.

"That's not what I meant," I groaned.

"Oh please don't insult me woman of God," Cornelius twitched as he mentioned the lord's name. "I am the most powerful being ever to live! I see all and I know all! I'm just having me a little fun." His malevolence lips widened to a sinister and horrifying grin.

"Why do you keep calling me a woman of god?" I almost hyperventilated as I spoke.

He cackled madly before composing himself and speaking.

"You're in a church aren't ya? Fighting demons aren't ya? Is *that* not doing the lords work? Is *that* not worthy of being called a woman of God?"

I gulped and didn't answer, but I did notice his twitches every time God was mentioned.

"Now, if I do this, then you will owe me a favour. Do we have a deal dear girl?" Cornelius said with an untrustworthy grin as he held out his hand.

"Do I have a choice?" I asked.

"Oh, silly-goose, everybody has a choice sweetheart, just make sure yours is the right one," -he replied in his evil and horrible voice whilst grinning his awful disgusting bloodcurdling grin.

I stood still, gathering my thoughts for a second; *do I really want to owe this monster a favour? -* I fretted – *But how else would we escape Vladimir and stop Jealousaw - and how else would I save my friends from the demons?*

"So, do we have a deal?" The scary man asked as he held out his frail hand.

Every fibre and instinct in my body told me no. But I needed to do something, I needed to save my friends!

"Deal" . . .

His grin widened to his eyes, "So be it. What do you desire sweetheart?"

"Explain to me how you know so much, but yet still don't know who told me your name?" I asked.

He seemed agitated suddenly, "No time for chit-chat!" He snapped, "Now tell me!"

"I want to know what you'll want in return, before I make any deals," I barked.

"You stupidly already shook on it and muttered the word 'deal.' We are bound in a magical contract now. Besides, I told you, it will be a favour," he grinned as he held out an open palmed hand.

"What favour?"

"Well I haven't thought of it yet!!!" He growled angrily making me jump. "Now, this is your last chance to save your friends before I abandon you! If you don't offer me anything verbally that you want, then you are in breach of your contract and I can still claim my end of it. Tell me what you want or leave your friends to their own fate!"

"I want to fulfil my potential. All of it. So that I can defend my friends and family!" I asked.

Cornelius raised a curious eyebrow . "You seek power? Perhaps you are your father's daughter," he grinned wickedly.

"How do you know my father?" I grumbled.

"Oh you'll find out soon enough," he sniggered as he clapped his hands. "Your potential is now fulfilled . . . Time Aristocrat!"

"What?" I gasped.

Cornelius rolled his eyes.

"You'll now have all the knowledge of an experienced Time Aristocrat. All your magical ability is fulfilled and you'll just know how to naturally use it, when the time is right. Your physical training abilities are fulfilled also. So those sparing lessons with Luscious Linx are no longer required. Don't worry, I won't tell him," Cornelius winked. "Don't be mistaken though Eleni. Your physical potential, just like sword fighting, can only go as far as the teacher's ability who taught you. Therefore, there is always room for improvement should you find a better instructor. Bear that in mind when you cross blades with Jealousaw!" He warned.

"And what about Vladimir?" I asked.

"What about him?" He chuckled.

"How do I escape this church from him?"

"You're a fully trained Warlock now my dear. One who is certainly powerful enough to deal with a measly vampire. Now, remember this from Uncle Cornelius, magic comes with a price! What that price is depends on what you do with it. Magic is linked to emotion. Good-willed magic tires you out and drains your power after a while, so you'll need rest. Hate-magic makes you less tired but not very likeable. Think of it like Star Wars. You have the dark side of the force and the light side of the force. You have the ability to go either way depending on your choices with your newfound abilities. Good luck Eleni. I'll be coming for that favour very soon," And with that he vanished and I was back in the room with Linx. Dread suddenly filled me as I realised what I had just done. I made a deal with a devil!

13- SLEEPY TIME

"Are you ok?" Linx gasped. "You zoned out there for a few minutes."

My entire body was trembling and I couldn't speak. My blood had turned to ice. His strong arms wrapped around me, burying me into his hard chest. I hadn't realised I was crying until his hands were rubbing my back as I sobbed.

"Hey, it's ok. Whatever it is we can deal with it," he said comfortingly.

"No, it's not ok," my voice jittered. The image was burned into my brain – that evil grin and those soulless eyes.

"What's happened, Eleni?" Linx asked as he cradled me even tighter.

"I made a deal with The Burned Soul," hysteria bubbled through me as I couldn't control my floods of tears.

His grip on me loosened and he pulled back from me to look at my face.

"You did what?" He gasped mortifyingly.

"He came to me. Cornered me. I wasn't sure where I was or if I even *had* a choice," I sobbed as I collapsed pathetically into him. He caught me and once again embraced me in his warm clutch.

"I'm scared Linx. I'm *really* scared!" My voice hitched as I begun to choke and not breathe I was crying so much.

I closed my eyes and cuddled against his warm chest. There was no other place I'd rather be. His heart beat steadily, calming me a little. I felt safe in his firm hold.

"It's ok baby, it's ok!" He kissed the top of my head and hugged me so tight. "It's ok, don't cry baby, please don't cry," he kept kissing my head.

His citrus smell flooded my nose and I glanced into his warm blue-green eyes. My emotions were rolling about inside of me like tumbleweed in a desert. I felt really awkward now that he had witnessed my full blown meltdown. How embarrassing, he must be so desperate to get away from a train wreck like me.

"I'm sorry," I tried to say but another irritating cry stole my words.

He pulled my head to his shoulder and I didn't resist. I laid my head right into his collarbone, enjoying the closeness. The silence descended between us, and fatigue hit me like a sledge hammer suddenly. The horror of meeting 'The infamous Burned Soul', had taken a lot out of me. I breathed in Linx's gorgeous scent. It was unique but lovely. Despite feeling calmer I still couldn't stop the whimpering as the sobs built back up.

"Don't cry baby," he whispered softly, "I'm here."

He continued to kiss my head over and over. First the top of my head as my face was buried in his hard chest, but as I leaned up to look at him he begun kissing my forehead as he held me.

"What are we going to do?" I blubbered. My nose was getting snotty, my eyes stung and my face was soaked from tears.

He placed his forehead to my forehead as he held my head cupped in both his hands. I could now feel his hot breath on my face.

"I don't know?" He whispered, "but I'm not going to let any harm come to you, I promise." His forehead pressed firmly against my forehead as he spoke with grit-determination.

I begun to cry again and he hushed me, still holding my head with both his hands and kissing my forehead.

"Don't cry." He pushed a piece of my hair behind my ear, and a jolt of hot electricity warmed my body. "I'll always protect you," his words were a promise and I liked them way too much. He didn't remove his hand, and it felt just for a moment like we were the only two people in the world. His touch felt really good and I found myself stepping further into him and he didn't back away. It felt like the jolt of electricity connected us now, making me crave him more. My eyes flicked to his lips and his to mine.

"You can't always protect me, Linx," I sighed as tears still rolled down my cheeks, "You can't be around all the time."

"I can try," he whispered.

Then, without warning his hot breath mixed with my breath. He edged closer. My heart stopped, as his warm hard lips pressed very softly against mine. A shock hit me hard like a voltage, I think he felt it too, but it didn't hurt, it felt quite the opposite. It was so pleasant I almost moaned as it jolted through us. He tasted of chocolate, which caught me off guard, and I never wanted to taste anything else ever again. The kiss was instinctive and unexpected from both of us. He just did it - *I* just did it. He kissed me and I kissed him back - it was an accident. I knew he hadn't meant to do it; he just naturally did it out of raw animal instinct. In the heat of the moment it took control as he held my whimpering sad head and was kissing my forehead so much - and then it sort of just happened. What neither of us was prepared for though, was my response. Before he could detach his warm moist mouth from mine, blood boiled under my skin and burned through my lips to his. My breath came in untamed gasps. My fingers wildly clawed and knotted in his hair, pinning him to me. My lips parted as I ate his face passionately. He immediately pulled back with a gasp, breaking the bridge of saliva that had formed between us.

"Oops," I breathed.

"What just happened?" He whispered in a disbelieving sigh, but his eyes were wild and his jaw clenched in acute restraint.

"You kissed me," I gasped as I bit my lip. His face mirrored my shocked expression.

"I'm sorry," he murmured, "I shouldn't have done that, I don't know why I did that," he turned from me and walked quickly out of the room.

I stood in disbelief for a few moments, my tears completely gone now. Suddenly I felt a little lightheaded – overwhelmed by meeting The Burned Soul and now snogging Linx - and I toppled to the floor. I hadn't heard him re-enter the room, but he must have heard me fall as suddenly I was cradled in his strong arms.

"Are you alright?" He gasped with panic.

"I don't know Linx, I went a little woozy," I managed to somehow respond.

My breath hitched again as I realised now as I gazed up at Linx, that I was truly and utterly besotted by him. His short black hair with the grey shining through on the sides, his stubbly chin, strong features and bulging muscles. He was just aw-so-mouth-watering-perfect and he dazzled me. There was no doubt about it that I fancied Indira. Who wouldn't? And there was no doubt in my mind that Lingwood was gorgeous and had the bad boy allure to him, but Linx I wanted. I wanted him so bad.

"Woozy," he chuckled, "I have that affect on all the women," he teased as he winked at me.

I managed to roll my eyes with a smirk as he helped me up. I was so glad that he was making light of it now so that we could both quickly forget about it. He obviously and clearly hadn't meant to do it and felt uncomfortable – and, I felt embarrassed too. Especially as I had practically glued *his* face to mine with the way my jaw clamped shut - sucking him in and locking my chops around his mouth. And the way I rustled through his hair so passionately, he must surely think that I was really desperate to be that full on with our first kiss. So, to spare both our blushes, it's best to make a joke and move on from our shame – except, my lips still tingled. And my heart still pulsed blood around my body faster than the river-rapids, as it sloshed about and caused turbulence within me. Butterflies still flapped around my stomach and I still felt dizzy.

"The Lynx affect," I mimicked the spray-can advert.

"Very funny!" He groaned as he playfully punched my arm.

I was so relieved that we weren't awkward around each other and were giving each other banter.

"We need to get back down the mountain," I stated firmly but wobbled slightly as I walked past him.

It appeared that I was intoxicated, not by the booze that I had consumed last night, but by Linx's very presence. His reactions were good as I stumbled. His arm shot out and snared around my waist. I flung into his hold and his still-swollen ankle gave way, sending us both tumbling to the floor in a heap. I found myself on top of him and for a second we were both entranced in the same mental fog, as our eyes locked firmly.

Finally we both laughed when Linx broke the tension. "I hope that's your belt digging into me," he joked as my hips mounted him, it's not like I pushed my hips down on purpose and

deliberately saddled him as though I was riding Fiona . . . *Well
. . .* maybe slightly.

I raised and lowered my eyebrows, "Maybe I'm just happy to
see you," I flirted.

He smiled invitingly, and then frowned and his grin quickly
faded "No, seriously?" He moaned.

"It's my belt!" I laughed, "But I can feel something too."

"Shut up!" He snickered as he playfully rolled me over.

"Get off!" I teasingly tried to kick him, but his bodyweight was
firmly in-between my legs and I immediately found my mind
in the gutter. Now I really could feel something and Linx
looked a little flushed. He went to get off of me and I rapidly
closed my thighs, trapping him light-heartedly.

"Let me go!" He said firmly but with a smirk.

I could feel him press against me now and I wished we could
have stayed locked in this position forever.

Then he said something that made my legs instantly open -
and not in the good-kinda-way. "We need to get out of this
church and back to Stadley Hold."

I released him and he staggered up, hobbling on one foot
before extending his arm out to me. I grabbed his hand and
something sparked between us where our skin touched -
similar to the jolt that struck when we kissed - the surge was
strong, but not unpleasant. Once he had helped me up I
quickly wiped my hand on my jeans, it still tingled from where
the static electricity had jolted between us.

"How's your ankle?" I asked.

"I'll live!" He replied as he hobbled out of the room.

The gates to Hell rattled furiously as I stepped past. I daren't even look as I held my breath until we were firmly away from them.

"So, how are we going to get past Vladimir?" Linx enquired.

"The Burned Soul told me that I'm powerful enough to deal with him," I explained.

"You can't trust *him*!" Linx asserted.

"Well, we have little choice!" I spat back as I marched past him and out into the church garden.

Vladimir was still stood where we had left him yesterday. His blood-red eyes darkened to a black when he saw me.

"Your father murdered my daughter, Eleni!" Vladimir growled.

"Wha?" I gasped, bewildered.

"Of course you and your friends, and even Linx here, don't remember. Your father has weakened the power stones dramatically by wiping your minds. All because he can't be bothered to pick up the pieces and explain things to you. Now, I will get revenge by killing *you*. A daughter for a daughter, an eye for an eye, if you like!" Vladimir snarled furiously.

"You can't touch us on Holy soil!" Linx spat.

"You can't stay there forever. You'll have to come out eventually and I'll be waiting. Meanwhile the demons are destroying Stadley Hall thanks to the weakened magic from *your* father's memory warping spell!" The vampire roared.

"What do you mean? What memory spell?" I needed to know.

"My daughter and I kidnapped you and were going to feast on your blood, but Indira and your father saved you from us thanks to your friends. I got away and they never knew I was even there, but my daughter wasn't so lucky. He murdered her!" Vladimir was enraged. "I've waited patiently for this opportunity to get you alone where your deaths can be blamed on the demons!"

"Why would my father warp mine and everybody else's memories?" I questioned.

"Because, it makes his life easier and spares *you* his *precious* daughter, a painful memory. But the cost of his spell has left Stadley Hall almost defenceless, and that is why the demons are taking full advantage. Stadley Hall will fall. And Earth will be destroyed, all thanks to your father. And my kind will rise from the ashes!" His face turned to a sickening grin.

"I won't let that happen!" I stepped closer to him.

His face changed to an expression of shock. "Something is different about you, child" He sniffed the air.

"Yeah it is!" I raged and suddenly a ghostly Cornelius Strumple appeared in my vision. Vladimir and Linx both couldn't see him, but I could.

"Hold your hand out open-palmed my young apprentice," the ghost that nobody else could see but me, instructed.

I did as I was told.

"Now, with all your rage and anger, clench that fist and imagine dragging that Vampire onto the holy land!" Cornelius snarled.

I clenched my fist angrily and pictured in my mind – Just like The Burned Soul instructed, *Vladimir being tugged onto the holy land*. Within an instant the dark figure of Vladimir Putin lurched forward as though he were pushed.

"NOOOOOOOOOOOOOO!!!!!" He yelped as he sizzled.

"Now hold him there with your mind!" Cornelius ordered.

I nodded and obeyed and Vladimir tried to scramble away but couldn't as my mind-power clamped his legs to the ground.

"What dark sorcery is this?" The Vampire hissed as he slowly burned.

"You are shackled by me, you monster!" I yelled with fury.

"This is for *my* parents!" Linx unexpectedly yelled as he pulled out his sword and swung it towards Vladimir's head. Linx's momentary emotional yell as he sliced his sword through the air, broke my concentration, which yielded my magic.

Vladimir swooped upwards, grabbing Linx's sword in mid-swing with both his hands, forcing it from his grip. Linx's eyes fell upon mine as he gasped, his face full of shock and sorrow as Vladimir slowly pushed the sword through his stomach.

"NOOOOOOOOOOOOOOO!!!!!!" I screamed as Linx collapsed to the floor, his gorgeous face now twisted with torment and suffering.

I threw Vladimir to the ground with all my rage-magic and kept him there sizzling. I turned to Linx who begun toppling over.

"I'm sorry Little E," he coughed as he fell to his knees.

My heart seized and coldness fell upon me, my knees went to jelly and my chest hurt as though it were being trampled by a thousand elephants.

"Please no, please no, please no!" My words hurt as they wheezed out of my weeping mouth. I buckled to the floor next to his limp body as I held him tight to my chest. Tears dropped like a waterfall from my gushing eyes as I howled.

"I'm sorry," he whispered.

I tried to keep his eyes open by making him laugh.

"Did you know Reverend Crone is a secret drag queen?" I laughed as tears rolled from my eyes.

He smirked for a second, then repeated in a breathless whisper, "I'm sorry."

"No, this is not the end," I disagreed under my breath.

His eyes were probing as he studied me for the last time, "Sleepy time now Little E," he begun to cough.

"Please stay with me," I whispered through the torture, stuttering each painful word.

He tried to smile, "You're the last of us now, Stone Chaser," his expression changed, softened and saddened by the subtle ache in my voice. "Eleni," his fingers lightly traced the shape of my

lips. I smiled under his fingertips, "Keep an eye out for Harry."
I touched his face, and his eyes slowly shut
 "Sleepy time now Little E."

THE END

+++EPILOGUE+++

-TROJAN HORSE-

"You've still not found Lukamore?" The dark figure snarled as he snapped General Looms neck – producing a sickening crunch.

"Receiving message now, my lord," Captain Harner gulped as he tried not to look at the dead body of his superior officer that now lay next to him, as he gazed respectfully up at Jealousaw, who loomed above him like a black-robed, omnipotent god.
"Good!" Jealousaw's deep voice boomed coldly, "Patch it through to my chamber!"
"Yes my lord," the captain swallowed nervously.

Every crew member fell silent as the dreaded and familiar heavy footsteps echoed through the corridor of the ship as the towering and much feared Jealousaw stomped to his private chamber.

"You've earned their trust?" Jealousaws deep and terrifying-distorted voice hissed.

"I have. They don't expect a thing. Stadley Hold's defences will be down very shortly once I steal the last of their power stones."

"And the girl?" Jealousaws chilling voice stained the air.

"She'll be all yours, my master."